NEXT!

100 Audition Monologues
by
Jason Milligan

Also Contains:
GUIDELINES FOR A
SUCCESSFUL AUDITION

IMPORTANT BILLING AND CREDIT REQUIREMENTS

All producers of NEXT! *must* give credit to the Author of the Play in all programs distributed in connection with performances of the Play and in all instances in which the title of the Play appears for purposes of advertising, publicizing or otherwise exploiting the Play and/or a production. The name of the Author *must* also appear on a separate line, on which no other name appears, immediately following the title, and *must* appear in size of type not less than fifty percent the size of the title type.

FOREWARD

If you sell kitchen sinks and garbage disposals for a living, your calling card is apt to read "plumbing supplies" underneath your name. If you're an actor, however, *you* are the commodity, and when you walk into an audition, you're, in essence, selling *yourself*. It is important to remember that you are a truly unique individual, different from everyone else, and *that's* what makes you a valuable commodity.

I've taught monologue workshops across the country, and I always advise my students to pick an audition monologue which says, "this is who I am." An actor's best resource is to have such a monologue on hand at all times, fully rehearsed and ready to perform at the drop of a hat – your very own "calling card," if you will. Performing this audition monologue is often the first impression you convey to prospective producers and/or directors, so I suggest that you have your "calling card" monologue ready to go when they call "Next!"

Now, don't feel restricted by the "Men" and "Women" divisions in this book. If you're an actress and you happen to find a piece in the "Men" section which you feel suits you well, by all means – use it. This book is meant to serve as a toolbox, and the monologues are the wrenches, the pliers, and the hammers. Use the tools you need to get the job done – or, in this case, to get the job.

In the back of this book is an appendix of *Guidelines for a Successful Audition.* I've compiled it using feedback from various auditors. I hope you find it helpful.

Break-a-leg!

Jason Milligan
Los Angeles, 1996

MONOLOGUES FOR WOMEN:

MONOLOGUES FOR MEN:

MONOLOGUES
FOR WOMEN

NEXT!

ALWAYS A PRICE TAG

What's the catch? *(Pause)* I mean, "what's the catch?" *(Pause)* Well, here you are, offering me a brand-new microwave oven, and I'm just wondering if there are any, you know ... *strings* attached. *(Pause)* Uh-huh ... Okay, then, is there anything *wrong* with it? *(Pause; the other person presumably starts laughing.)* What's so *funny*? Huh? I'm *serious*! I mean, like, is the *door* not on good and the rays are gonna come leaking out and make my hair fall out when I heat-up my coffee? Or, or, is the wiring shot and it's going to make my house burn down when I cook a TV dinner? *(Pause as the other person assures her that nothing is wrong with the microwave.)* You're *sure*? Mm-hmm ... *(Pause)* Y'know, my grandmother always used to tell me, "you don't get something for nothing in this world." And she was always right about things. Now, I'm looking at this oven and I'm thinking, boy I sure could use it ... but I'm not clear as to what the "price" is – and I'm not sure if I want to *pay* the price! There's gotta be a price tag, Clifford. There's *always* a price tag. Always. For everything in this world. And if there's *not*, like if you go into some fancy restaurant where there aren't any prices on the menu, watch out! Because if you don't see any prices, then you *know* you're in trouble! 'Cause when they purposely *don't* show you the price, you know it's gonna be sky-high. Now, I don't see any prices on this particular item, so I want to know: if I take this, am I going to regret it? *(Pause)* You're the kind of person, Clifford, who likes to have people in their debt. *Owing* you. Do you know what I'm saying? Because I do not want to be in your "debt," and I do not want to "owe" you anything. So you tell me, and you tell me the truth: what's the catch?

BORN LOSER

I love Ed. And I know he loves me with an undying, eternal devotion. But I swear, sometimes he's just a Born Loser. See, it all started when I said to him one day, "I wish we could buy a house." Now, I should've known better than to plant that seed in that sweet little pea-brain of his. Because t'weren't long before he went out and robbed an armored car from the First National Bank to try and get the down payment for a mobile home! Held the driver up at gunpoint and grabbed the first four bags of money he could lay his hands on. For *me*! I know he was doin' it all for me. Only ... he'd parked his "getaway car" in a no-parking zone and it got towed during the holdup. And the bags he stole, they were all *pennies*, and they were so heavy that they slowed Ed down and the police nabbed him about a block and a half from the scene of the crime. *(Pause) Then*, after he got sent up to the Work Farm, I made the mistake of tellin' him that I was scared at night. So he got it into his head that t'weren't safe for me to be all alone out here while he was doin' time. So he broke out one night and ran almost all the way here. Twenty-three miles! Only ... he got sprayed by a skunk before he got off the Work Farm, and, well, with a smell like that, t'weren't long before the dogs tracked him down. Six blocks from our driveway! He was so close ... So, as you know, they doubled his time and took away his chances for parole. Poor Ed ... you see what I mean? Born Loser. He's not a criminal by nature. He's not even a good criminal at *all*, period! The thing is, see, he was doin' all this for *me*. So maybe you kind folks on the parole board could take this into consideration when you look into Ed's situation. I promise I'll take really good care of him if you'll let him out early. And I won't ask him for anything, ever again, as long as I live! You've got my word on it.

CIVILIZED

Do that again. Do – no, I mean: *(Sticks tongue out, then grimaces, reacting in a disgusted manner.)* Ugh! What *is* that? What do you mean, *"what?"* In your *tongue*! Sticking *through* your tongue! That's what I *thought*! You mean to tell me, you went out and had your *tongue* pierced? Who in their right mind does something like that? Untamed natives on an uncharted desert isle? Maybe ... Runaway kids with spiked purple hair on Sunset Boulevard? Maybe ... But not *you*, Bruce. You're *civilized*! You have a $100,000-a-year job! You drive a BMW! You own a condo on the beach! You speak four languages and you were a Rhodes Scholar, you are not the kind of individual who walks around with a little stainless steel spear sticking through his tongue! Next thing you're going to tell me, you're going back to get a *bone* put through your nose! *(Pause; reacts in shock.)* NO! Oh my God, Bruce ... *(Becomes reflective:)* You think you know somebody and then, all of a sudden, they throw you for a loop! *(Reacts as "Bruce" moves closer.)* No, no! I don't want to "touch" it. What? *No!* I don't want to *kiss* you, either! Yeah, well, you should've thought of that before you went out and *perforated* yourself. *(Pause; softens a little:)* Oh, Bruce, I'm sorry. I love you, I really *do* ... it's just ... well, it's really hard to imagine you with a bone through your nose. I mean, when you sneeze, which way does it go? *(Ponders this for a brief moment, then:)* But, then again, I guess it pretty much guarantees you being the center of attention at your high school reunion. *(An idea suddenly dawns on her:)* Wait a minute ... is *that* why you did this? So that you'd be "noticed?" Bruce, honey. There are other ways to be noticed. Ways which are – I promise you – a *lot* simpler. So if you'll take out that spear, I promise we'll sit down and think of some ... *together*.

COLUMNS

They're *people*, Mr. Clark. Everyone here, they're all human beings. And they deserve to be treated as such. But you have this *way* about you, I dunno ... How you "categorize" people. You say to yourself, "he's an idiot," and you write him off into Column A: The Idiot Column. Or "she's a good employee, a good worker," so you protect her, you put her in Column B: The Good Worker Column. Or you think, "I'd like to get *that* one into bed," so she immediately gets labeled a sex object and goes right into Column C: The Sex Object Column – do not pass "Go," do not collect $200 – with all the rest of the sex objects who work here wearing those short little skirts, dreaming that they're going to get promoted one day. But of course they're not ever going to get promoted, are they? They're in Column C: The Sex Object Column, not Column B: The Good Worker Column. Do you see a *pattern* here? Do you see what I'm trying to say? Up 'till now, I've been pretty lucky – I've been in Column B: The Good Worker Column since the day I started working here. But one wrong move, one wrong step, and – *boom!* I could end up in the wrong column. I told somebody – a friend, who, incidentally, is in Column A: The Idiot Column – that I was going to come up here and have this talk with you, and she warned me, she said, "but he *likes* you! Don't rock the boat!" But I can't take it anymore. Sitting back and watching the way you treat some of these people? And I know I'm on the "good list." But it doesn't feel so "good" when all around you, everywhere you look, people are being humiliated. I don't care if this hurts my status or bumps me into the wrong column. Because your columns don't mean a thing to me, Mr. Clark. I just want you to realize how you treat people. And how it makes them feel.

CRAMPING MY STYLE

I used to hate it when Wally went out on the road. Days, weeks at a time, he'd be off, hauling manure or sidewalls or chain link fences to Topeka ... Portland ... Austin ... you name it, he's been there. *(Pause)* Well, like I said, I used to hate being left alone here all by myself. But after awhile, I started to get *used* to it. And then, after awhile longer, I started to *like* it! Matter of fact, I started to love Wally being away even more than him being *here*! All the things he hated, I could go out and do while he was gone – I could go to the movies, go to church, go out for long walks in the desert ... I even started a bowling league with some of the girls down at the beauty salon, we won the division championship last year! *(Pause)* So, as you can see, it's kind of hard for me right now. Wally just had to go and get that hernia, changing a flat on his rig outside Santa Fe. Doctor said he needs to stay in bed for *three weeks.* "Complete Bed Rest." So now he's here 24 hours a day, and he expects *me* to wait on him hand and foot! I don't know what I'm gonna do, Emma ... I swear, if he hollers for me to go fetch him a cold beer *one more time,* I'm afraid I'm gonna do something drastic! I dunno, like bash him in the head with my skillet! And I'm talkin' about my *good* skillet too, so you know I mean business! *(Pause as she calms herself again.)* I dunno ... I reckon I'd expect him to take care of me if *I* was ever to get sick like this ... but if only he *knew* how bad he was cramping my style!

EASY WAY OUT

If you were blindfolded, flown to any major city in America, and deposited in the middle of a shopping mall, you'd have no way of knowing where in God's name you were. There'd be a McDonald's, a Gap, a Pottery Barn, a Williams-Sonoma, JC Penny ... blah, blah, blah. This whole country has sold it soul for the sake of redevelopment. We've become one giant hodgepodge of *sameness,* everywhere you look. I mean, whatever happened to all those Mom-and-Pop businesses that used to flourish? You hardly ever see those anymore. Towns like this one, they're all losing their individuality. Little by little, they're all being swallowed up by a monster Big Mac with an unsatiable appetite. *(Pause)* Well, I'm sorry if I sound like I'm on my soapbox again. I just can't believe what I'm hearing! Fred is willing to stake you in *any restaurant* you want to open, and you're actually thinking about buying a fast food franchise? *(Pause)* I know, I know. It's a "cash cow," I saw the figures. But there's more to life than cash. Isn't there? I *love* this town, Stan. Don't you? Don't you want our kids to grow up in the same All-American Apple Pie place that *we* did? *(Pause)* No, you're right. One fast food place *isn't* going to destroy Willow Falls. But it's an Easy Way Out, Stan. That's what it is. And too many people are taking the Easy Way Out these days. Too many. It's eroding any sense of character that towns like this once had. Don't you *want* to live in a cute little hamlet that's not like any other place in the whole world? Or do you want to be the one to pave the way for an onslaught of sameness? You decide.

FALSE CLAIMS

All my life, people have told me that I'm stupid. Or that I'm sickly ... that I'd never amount to anything ... all my life! And, used to be, I never knew any better, so I just believed them. Believed I couldn't ever achieve anything. Believed I'd always be a nobody. Believed I'd be in and out of hospitals for the rest of my life – I bought it all – hook, line and sinker. But I want to tell you something: those are all just false claims. And I realize that I don't have to accept them any more. You sell insurance, Deanna. You know what I'm talking about. If a claim comes in and you think it's false, you reject it. Well, the idea that I'm *sickly* is a false claim. Look at me: I'm not sickly! I'm running two miles a day now! When I was listening to all that crap about how sick I was, I couldn't gasp one breath for fear of, what, "asthma?" Whatever. And the whole notion that I'm stupid is a false claim too. I'm not stupid. Look. *(Points)* Over there, in that frame. That is my *diploma*, Deanna, Ten years late, but that is my high school diploma. I never thought I would ever have one, I never believed it was even possible. Everybody was always telling me I wasn't "smart enough." *(Pause)* I am so proud of that little piece of paper, I don't know how to tell you. And do you know why? Because it means that all those claims about me, all those years, were false claims. All I have to do is shake them off from now on. One by one.

FAR TOO GULLIBLE

You're *not* serious. *(Looks at something – a document – that's being offered by the other person)* Oh, no! Wilbur ... *(Shakes her head sadly)* I think you just may have made a *huge mistake*. No, no, I understand that the rates they offered you were incredible, I understand *that*! Did you ever stop to think that maybe the rates were too good to be *true*? *(Pause)* How much money did you give these people? *("Wilbur's" response is a blow to her:)* Oh my God ... Wilbur. Yeah, well, there's probably a good reason nobody's ever heard of "Blackjack Investment Opportunities" before. Because if we try to follow up on this, I'm sure they'll be gone. Poof. Vanished. Disappeared from the face of the earth. *(Pause)* No, I'm not mad ... just tired. Tired of all these people preying on you like a bunch of vultures. They can see you coming a mile away. You're too trusting, Wilbur. You're – no, that's not the right word ... gullible. That's it. That's the whole problem: you are far too gullible for your own good. *(Pause)* That great plumbing job the guy talked you into? *(Pause)* Sure, if you like cold showers. Personally, I prefer hot ones. No, no, don't call him again, he'll take you for another two grand! And we might as well have a running tab with the mechanic. Every time you take the car into the shop, he talks you into eight, nine hundred dollars' worth of repairs! *(Pause)* Well, maybe now you'll learn. Maybe now you'll see what happens when you listen to strangers. These big schemes that are too good to be true! Why, I'll bet you'd jump right now if some guy came up and said he had a brand-new Mercedes to sell you for $500. *(Pause, then scolds Wilbur:)* Wilbur! You see what I mean? You're *far too gullible!*

FINE TOOTH COMB

Mrs. Weatherby? Hi, you remember me? It's Darlene. *(Pause)* Darlene Crenshaw? I sold you that pie at the Episcopal Church bake sale yesterday. Rhubarb pie, that's right! Well, I'm sorry to come over here and ring your doorbell so early on a Sunday morning, but I have to know ... have you, by any chance ... *eaten* any of the pie? *(Pause)* No? *(Relieved:)* Oh, praise the Lord! Well, then, if you'll just unhook your screen door and hand that pie out to me, I'll take it home and I'll bake you two more fresh ones for your trouble. *(Pause. Her face falls:)* WHAT? He *what*? You mean, *the whole thing*? Your husband ate the *ENTIRE PIE*? Well, it's a *whole pie*, Mrs. Weatherby, no *wonder* he's so fat! *(Corrects herself:)* I mean, large. *(Corrects herself again:)* I mean ... *big*? Ooh, I'm sorry, Mrs. Weatherby. I don't mean to insult you *or* your husband, it's just – well ... it's like this: I baked six pies for the bake sale, and we sold three, and I got the other two back last night, and so you're the only person with an outstanding pie. I dug through all the other pies, and – well, the long and short of it is, *my engagement ring was buried in your pie*! I'm positive! It must've slipped off my finger while I was making the pies, when I was scooping out the filling, and like I said, I've already been through the other five pies with a fine-tooth comb, so we may need to take Mr. Weatherby to the hospital and have his stomach pumped if he really ate the whole thing, because my ring was in that pie somewhere! *(Sits, hot and flustered, fanning herself with her hand:)* Oh, I'm sorry ... I'm so very sorry ... it's just that my fiancee – Eddie – he will *never* understand how I lost the engagement ring he took two years to save up for. And if I tell him I lost it in a Rhubarb Pie ... well, I just know he'll never forgive me 'cause he hates Rhubarb Pie more than anything else in this whole entire *world*! *(Pause)* Oh, would you? Thank you *so* much ... I'll wait right out here, and you just stick your finger down Mr. Weatherby's throat and you give me a holler if anything shiny comes up.

FREE RIDE

What, then? Huh? Will you just *tell* me? Do you want me to give you a ride home? Do you need some money? What? What? WHAT? *(Pause; calms herself.)* I'm sorry, Mark ... it's just, I've had it up to here with you always asking for "favors." I know, I know, Mom would be the first to say "do unto others," but I'm about ready to "do unto you" with a baseball bat! I got you a job at the Courthouse. Why aren't you down there? *(Pause)* It was not "too hard!" It was the easiest job in town! All you had to do was make sure the courtroom was tidy each morning. Sweep up a little bit, maybe dust once a week ... they were gonna pay you for an eight-hour day, and the most you'd ever have to work would be two or three hours. No, no, now don't hide behind that excuse, it's not that the Judge didn't like you, you just wanted another Free Ride, didn't you? All your life, you've latched onto other people's coattails and you've been given free rides. Well, it stops now. Right here. With me, anyway. Go find somebody else to latch onto. Not that you will, everybody else in this town is wise to you by now. *(Pause)* No, I'm *not* being cold! I'm trying to *help* you! By getting you to help yourself! *(Pause)* Well, I'm sorry if you see it that way, but that's how it is. I got you a job and you lost it. You go find another one yourself. I don't care anymore. *(Pause)* No, I take that back. I *do* care, Mark. That's why I can't stand back and watch you do this anymore. You have to take responsibility sometime. But I guess you're going to have to find that out on your own.

GARDEN VARIETY

No, I think Andy's a *great* guy. It's just ... *(Pause as she forms her thoughts:)* You know that old cliche, "never judge a book by its cover?" Well, I think that's true. Especially when it comes to people. Because sometimes, what's on the outside doesn't really indicate what's on the inside. What I mean ... *(Pause. Trying to explain:)* When I was a little girl, we had this garden. I remember, my Dad planted all these vegetables. And in no time, they started coming up like magic. Gorgeous-looking carrots ... plump potatoes ... We wanted to pick some right away, but Dad wouldn't let us. He wanted us to wait until everything was ripe. We were going to have our very own meal, cooked from our very own vegetables, picked from our very own garden. Anyway, when we finally got around to pulling the potatoes up ... they were all rotten inside. Maybe we'd waited too long or something, I don't know, maybe the soil was bad, but even though they looked great on the outside, they were black and rotten on the inside. Same thing with the carrots. Looked beautiful on the outside ... but inside they were rotten to the core. *(Pause)* No, I'm not saying that Andy is rotten to the core, I'm just saying ... Look, you've got to admit: on the outside, he puts on a really terrific facade. But on the inside ... I dunno. I think there's something dark and kind of ugly lurking somewhere beneath the surface. I just want you to be careful, that's all. I don't want to see you get hurt. And I have this weird feeling that he's the kind of guy who could hurt you. Big time.

GRACE

(Begins the piece seated; just a tiny bit tipsy at first, but she will grow progressively drunker and more slurred as the speech goes on:) I'm so glad you're all here on this lovely Thanksgiving ... let's bow our heads, why don't we, and Willard, you say grace. *(An irritated pause, then:)* All right, then. *I'll* say grace ... *(Bows her head:)* Heavenly Father, we thank you for this lovely Thanksgiving. This delicious feast before us ... we thank you for bringing my brother Billy and his girlfriend Kitty – *(Kitty's name, by the way, is said with great disdain.)* – safely home to us on this holiday ... even though they seem determined to live in *sin* for the rest of their lives! – *(Looks up, repentant:)* Oh, I'm sorry! I didn't mean that. I think maybe I might have had one too many cocktails today. Turkey took so long ... Three's my limit. *(Bows her head again:)* Anyway, thank you, God, for this lovely spread of food before us. The stuffing ... the deviled eggs ... the rolls ... And we realize that this may be our last substantial meal, what with Willard getting fired and everyth – *(Looks up again:)* What? Oh, I'm sorry, Willard. I'm sorry ... I slipped. Slightly. I suppose I slightly slipped. I know you didn't want that to get out today. *(Pause)* What? I said I was sorry! *(Starts to get up; her head is spinning, and she has to sit down again.)* Oh, my ... I simply cannot *drink* like this anymore. Remind me, Willard, five's my limit. Now, where was I? Oh, yes ... *(Bows head again:)* And we're so grateful to have Willard's mother here with us today. Ninety-two years old. But who's counting? *(Sudden violent burst of anger hurled at "Willard's Mom":)* WHEN ARE YOU GOING TO DIE, YOU OLD BUZZARD? ARE YOU GOING TO COME OUT HERE ON EVERY MAJOR HOLIDAY AND MAKE MY LIFE HELL FOREVER? *(Stops, composes herself.)* Oh. I don't know what's gotten into me ... Willard, you really must remember to remind me: nine's my limit. Well ... I guess it's time to carve the bird. Carve, Willard. Willard? *(Apparently, Willard says "no.")* WILLARD, *CARVE!* *(Willard begins to carve.)* Good. Now let's see, have I forgotten anything? Oh, yes ... *(Rises, staggering, as if to get another drink:)* Can I get anybody another drink?

GRIM CIRCUMSTANCES

(Addressing a small group:) All right, gentlemen ... Before we start the meeting, I would like to know who sent me the lovely xerox. *(Pause)* Someone in this room knows what I'm talking about, and I'm going to find out who it is. Now. Apparently one of you – a man with a grade school mentality, I might add – thought it would be simply hilarious to pull his pants down, sit on the xerox machine, and to send me the photocopy of his rump in an unmarked inter-office mail envelope. *(Pause, then directed to one "man" in particular:)* No, Carter, I *don't* think it's a "harmless joke." No. Because, you see, I have encountered resistance from you all ever since I took over this division. Why this resistance, I keep asking myself. It's not that I'm underqualified for the job, I'm *more* than qualified. And since I've been here, I've increased productivity by 75%. So it's not because I'm not doing a good job. It's because I'm a woman. Period. Isn't that right? *(Pause as she surveys the men.)* Well, let me say it once and for all: I'm sick and tired of all the lewd glances. I'm weary of all those little under-the-breath remarks. I want to know who did this, and I want to know now, because whoever it is ... is fired. That's all there is to it. *(Pause)* What, no one's going to take responsibility? Fine ... Then everyone against the wall now, and drop your pants. *(Pause)* Oh, I'm *dead* serious. No, no, no, not facing me. I'd rather you turned away. See, the genius who did this didn't stop to think that the tattoo on his left buttock – of a little nude mermaid, no less – would be noticed. Well, it *was* noticed. One of you has a tattoo on his left butt cheek. And as soon as I find out who it is ... they're out of a job. Now drop your pants, boys. I know you've been waiting to hear me say that since day one. Sorry it's under such grim circumstances.

HARD TO SHAKE

Every night when I'm lying in bed, I hear it go rumbling by: the bus. Whoever's driving nights, I'll say this for him, he's always right on time. Two-fifteen ... three-fifteen ... four-fifteen. Every hour at a quarter past. And somewhere around four-thirty, I finally fall asleep. But I tell you, it's awfully hard to fall asleep these days, especially when I keep hearing that bus right outside my bedroom window. I know, I know, you probably think I'm obsessing about it. But it's hard not to. I've been thinking about moving. Maybe it'd be a good change for me. I don't know ... *(Pause)* Bill used to take that same bus home from work every night. I couldn't go to sleep until he had gotten home. I'd lie there listening ... eleven-fifteen ... twelve-fifteen ... one-fifteen ... and then I'd hear his key in the lock. I couldn't fall asleep until I heard the one-fifteen hiss of the bus outside, opening its doors ... the doors closing ... and then Bill's key in the lock. *(Pause)* Then one night, two-fifteen ... three-fifteen ... four-fifteen ... no key in the lock. I called the plant, Joe Davis said "he left here at midnight like he always does." Around dawn the police came and told me. Two men shot Bill trying to take his wallet. Killed him. He didn't want to let go of that wallet because it had our wedding picture inside ... *(Has to stop and compose herself.)* I just get scared, that's all. Bill wasn't old, or sick or anything. One day he just left to go to work ... and he never came back. And, you see, whenever *you* leave ... oh, it's stupid, isn't it? But I can't help it. I get scared that something bad's going to happen to you too. It's hard to shake a feeling like this. It stays with you a long time.

HOT WATER

Jerome used to have this really irritating habit ... you see, he *hummed* whenever he chewed. *(Imitates it.)* It used to drive me up the wall! And he wasn't even *aware* that he was doing it. That's the whole point. I'd say, JEROME, SHUT UP! And he'd look at me as if I'd just told him I was a squid or something! I can only explain it as an unconscious seedling in his brain. Like a grain of sand in an oyster, causing an irritation. But, like an oyster, I eventually realized that Jerome's humming might one day produce a pearl. You see, even though it was insanely bothersome, it soon occurred to me that his humming was also marvelously original. That is to say, he was composing original tunes as he ate, without even *knowing* it! Jerome turned out to be a mindless Mozart, sculpting very marketable tunes as he chomped his corn on the cob. And deserts – deserts made him launch into an impromptu reggae dance beat! *(She dances a moment, then brings herself back to the subject at hand:)* So I went and bought a voice-activated tape recorder and I fastened it underneath Jerome's chair with duct tape. Within weeks, I had dozens of tunes, and I took them to a music publisher by the name of Stan Starr. *That* Stan Starr, yes. Well, over the course of six – no, I'm sorry, seven – months, we amassed quite a fortune by selling Jerome's songs. Only ... I never *told* Jerome about any of this. I was afraid that if I did, it might somehow wreck his unconscious composing talent, make it *impure* in some way. *(The point is:)* So you see, since I never told Jerome about the publishing deal, it's rather difficult to tell him about the seven million dollar *plagiarism suit* that's pending against him. It seems all the "tunes" I thought were so original weren't so original after all. He must've heard them on the radio, or the elevator, or God knows where. *(Pause)* I can't blame Jerome. It's not his fault. Oh, if only he'd taken up a *quiet* irritating habit instead ... like nail biting ... then I wouldn't be in all this hot water right now.

HUMAN BARNACLE

We have got to do something about George. *(The other person doesn't know who "George" is.)* George! *(Trying to clarify:)* George? Little guy with the goatee? *(Pause)* Yes! Yes, "that" George. Well, he's such a leech. No, no, not "lech," as in "sexual," he's not a deviant or anything like that, he's just leechy. Needy. He takes. He sucks your blood! No, not a vampire. He sucks *time*. He sucks the minutes of your life away from you, and never returns them. Sucks the life right out of you. George is one of Those People who corners you and he just starts talking and talking and he never stops, and he never lets you get a word in edgewise and it's not like a *conversation* – oh, no, God forbid! – it's like this endless monologue, this nonending vomitus torrent of words that flows from his mouth on and on and on, unceasing, like there's some sort of contest to see how long he can latch onto you and talk, talk, talk about nothing whatsoever that's interesting, and you can just feel the minutes of your life, the seconds, ebbing away, flowing away, ticking away – tick, tick, tick – he snatches them from you and they're gone – gone forever! *(Takes a breath, then continues:)* And you can't get *rid* of him! God forbid! You can't turn him off like you turn off a light switch – I wish to God you could – no, he latches onto you like this, this Human Barnacle, and he just starts talking and talking and going on and on and on until you think, oh my God, I'm going to scream! *(Looks up, sees something:)* Oh, no! Here he comes! Don't leave me with him! I don't know what I'll do if he starts TALKING!

IN YOUR HANDS NOW

So what if he couldn't speak Greek? Who speaks Greek anymore, anyway? Isn't that a dead language? Oh, that's *Latin*, you're right ... *(Pause, then shakes her head.)* I guess I just don't understand you, Clarice. I don't understand you at all anymore. I mean, every time I turn around, you're with somebody else. Now, what was wrong with Kurt? *(Pause)* Okay then, what about Ben? Ben was a terrific guy, why didn't you stick with him? *(Pause)* I see ... Well, do you think – *maybe* – that you're doing yourself a little *disservice* here, Clarice? Well, just for argument's sake, lets say that you've – *perhaps* – set your standards just a little bit ... *high*? Not every man you meet is going to speak nine different languages. And be proficient in water polo, lacrosse, boating, swimming *and* snorkeling. Oh, excuse me – "*scuba* diving." I didn't know there was a difference. *(Pause as "Clarice" tells her the difference.)* Oh, well, we can't forget the air tank, now can we? Clarice! Will you *listen* to yourself? You've turned into a *snob*! We always promised each other we'd speak up if one of us turned into a butt. Well, I think you've become a big fat butt! *(Looking down, as if at Clarice's rear end:)* No, no, I didn't say you *had* a big fat butt, I said you've turned *into* a big fat butt. I mean the way you look at things. You've just gotten to be so *judgmental*, Clarice. Well, *I* think so. Look, you've been through sixty-three boyfriends in the last twelve months, don't you think that's the sign of a *slightly* picky person? *(Pause)* Look, I promised you a long time ago that I would tell you if you ever became a jerk. So there. I've done my part. I've discharged my duty. I've spoken my piece. You do whatever you want ... it's in your hands now.

IVORY TOWER

(Start seated, very solemn, as if some grievous, momentous news has just been told:) I see. *(Pause)* Well, what do you want me to say? Would you feel better if I ranted and raved and called you names? *(Pause)* Well, I don't want you to feel "better," Howard. Besides, I knew this was coming, so it's not a big shock. Yeah, I've watched you come in here and fire everybody one by one and I knew it was only a matter of time before you got to me. *(Rises to go, then stops.)* What? "Don't tell anybody?" What are you gonna do if I *tell*? Huh? *Fire* me? Hah! I'm already fired! But – no. *(Calms herself.)* I don't want to get upset here. Because, in some perverse way, I think that would give you pleasure. And I do *not* want to give you any pleasure, Howard. *(Pause)* Y'know, I've watched you run this place smack into the ground. You fired all the good people. You don't know the first thing about running a firm like this. All you know how to do is can people. *(Smiles)* Well, the reason I'm not more upset is because I can see the Bigger Picture, Howard. Yeah. See, you've been a total jerk to everybody here. Fired working men – and women – with families to support ... but like I said, I can see the Bigger Picture. One of these days, you're going to pay for what you're doing. Oh, I may not be around to see it, but I know that your fall is going to be spectacular. Because you've put yourself up in such a high Ivory Tower. So enjoy the view while you can. It's a long way down.

KEEPING UP APPEARANCES

We didn't start *out* with all this. All we *used* to have, back when we started out, was that little one-bedroom apartment you rented us, a worn-out sofabed and that beat-up '73 Nova that leaked like a sieve whenever it rained. But the minute we started to make money ... things changed. Overnight. We suddenly inherited a whole new set of friends – friends with money – who drove Mercedes convertibles and lived in five-bedroom homes and belonged to the Country Club. Well, it wasn't long before we fell right in step with them. And our life became all about Keeping Up Appearances. It sounds so silly now, now that I have a little perspective, but it was very serious business then. We ran out and bought two brand-new cars – oh, and we couldn't own a car that was over a year old, we were trading in every time we turned around. And our house ... it's the kind of place a Sultan would live in! Not *us*! It's too much, Maggie. Way too much. Our life has become all about keeping up appearances ... and nothing more. So when I heard your one-bedroom was available again ... well, it seemed like our destiny! That's why I called. I say, to hell with Keeping Up Appearances ... I want to get back to living our lives again, like normal people. So ... does it still go for seven-fifty a month?

LIVING AMONG SAVAGES

Oh, the Blind Date? He was very ... interesting. *(Pause)* All right, let's not mince words: *disgusting's* more to the point. Not only did he eat with his fingers – and we're talking spaghetti and meatballs, Sid – but he had the most horrendous body odor I have ever smelled in my life! When he showed up at my apartment – before I even opened the door – I smelled him outside. I should've just hid and not answered the door. Or I should've said, "oh, you've got the wrong apartment," or something. That's my problem, I'm too damned nice! *(Shudders recalling the odor:)* Anyway, it was just unbearable once we got in his car ... I was sitting there choking, trying to hold my breath – but you can only hold your breath just so long. So I tried to roll down the window a little and breathe through the crack. I mean, I'd rather have polluted city air in my lungs any day of the week than the b.o. cloud! But he said, "it's cold outside. You want, I'll turn the heat up." It became this duel over the power window control, I'd roll it down, and he'd roll it up. And so there I was ... in this moving oven with his b.o. intensifying in the soaring temperature until my eyes were watering and I was practically asphyxiating right there in the passenger seat! *(Pause)* I did! I *did* ask him. I said, "Glum" – that was his name. Glum Cranston. "Glum, may I ask you a personal question? Do you ever use deodorant?" And he laughed and he said, "Never. The chicks really dig my manly smell." Can you believe it? "The chicks dig my manly smell!" *(Pause, then suddenly taken aback with great shock.)* What? You're *kidding*! <u>You</u> <u>too</u>? Oh my God ... but you're an educated guy, Sid! You're saying ... ? I don't believe what I'm hearing! I thought that at least *some* guys were intelligent. I thought that at least *some* guys were sensitive. Like *you*. But, no. You're all the same, aren't you? I'm living among savages! All of you! Like cavemen, you want to knock me in the head and drag me back to your cave and take advantage of me on the cold, damp earth. *(Pause; composes herself.)* I'm sorry ... I just never realized that some people place such a premium on unsavory smells. You have just lowered my faith in the male half of the human race, Sid. Lowered it by one big notch!

LIVING PROOF

My great aunt Luna is living proof of Divine Protection. You should see her: she drives this great big black '64 Lincoln Continental, and she careens up and down the streets of San Francisco without ever looking where she's going. Without ever using a turn signal ... flying through pedestrian crossings like a bat out of hell. You should see them leap out of the way as she zooms through intersections without the slightest glance left or right. Those poor cable car guys live in constant terror of that black Lincoln. But the kicker is, in 30 years of driving, she's never had an accident! Not one! How can you explain that? The only thing I can think of is Divine Protection. Some higher power that holds Luna firmly in its protective grasp as she hurtles forth, doing battle on the highways and byways of the Bay Area in her car like an ancient Roman chariot of war. *(Pause)* Well, if Luna can be held in the grasp of divine protection, so can you. *(Pause)* I know, I know, you're scared ... I would be too. But forget about *you* for a second, okay? Take *you* out of the picture. And just think about Luna. Just keep thinking about Luna and how she's protected and I promise you, you'll be fine.

LOOKALIKE

It's come in handy looking like a famous person. You *do* know who I look like, don't you? *(Turns to offer a profile, strikes a pose. It doesn't really matter if you really look like anybody famous, just play the monologue as if you do:)* People stop me on the street all the time and say, "aren't you – ?" *(Other person asks "really?")* Oh, Yeah ... Yeah, it's gotten me in quite a few doors. Into the fanciest restaurants. The hottest nightclubs ... *(A not-so-cheery memory:)* ... it's also landed me in a whole heap of trouble. See, when I went to New York last month on business, I thought it might be fun to check into my hotel under the name of – yeah. Just to *see*. Well, I get to my room and there's baskets of fruit and champagne, room service – all "on the house." And I'm thinking, "this is great, I should've tried this a long time ago!" That's when there's a knock on the door and these two Federal agents show up. Drag me out of the room in handcuffs, shove me into a big black car, and drive me downtown. And I'm terrified. I'm thinking, they're going to lock me up and throw away the key for impersonating a celebrity! *(Pause)* Well, that's the kicker: Income Tax Evasion. *(Nods)* Uh-huh ... *(Then shakes her head in response to what the other person just asked.)* No, not *me. Her*! I know, can you imagine? A big celebrity like that? No, no, I finally straightened it all out, I told them who I really was. But my advice to you is, if you want to pretend you're some famous person ... check 'em out first. And make sure it's not somebody who owes five million bucks to the government!

LOVE AND AUTO MECHANICS

Well, that's kind of hard to explain ... it all started when I had to take my car into the shop. See, I bought a Volvo. Now, I didn't know much about foreign cars – well, let's face it: I didn't know *anything* about *any* cars, period! I hated it when I had to take the car into the shop because those mechanics would prey on my ignorance. All those sweat-stained coveralls and greasy grubby hands and it's this Male Thing – I'm a woman and they try to shut me out. They'd launch into all this macho "lingo" about cars and engines and manifolds and I'd have to keep asking, "so what are you saying? What's the problem?" And they'd say, "oh, it's the transmission." Or, "it's the engine." Something that sounded daunting – I didn't know any better. I mean, as soon as they even opened the hood, I was lost. Next thing I know, they're handing me a bill for $1,200 and the car still isn't running right. Was I taken advantage of? I don't know. *(Pause)* Mom always imagined I would end up marrying a doctor or a corporate lawyer or someone of that ilk. But I think I was attracted to Bud because ... honestly? He knew about cars. I first laid eyes on him crawling out of the pit at the Mobil station and it was like he was the one who could unlock this unfathomable mystery for me. He could explain it all to me. He could make me feel less ignorant, less self-conscious, more sure of myself. I mean, let's face it: I never dreamed I'd end up with an auto mechanic either. But if you could see the look Bud gets on his face whenever he's doing an oil change ... *(Swoons)* And I tell you, now I'm never afraid to take my car to the garage anymore. Thanks to Bed, now I know more about that Volvo than any of *them*!

MAGIC INGREDIENT

Is there some magic ingredient that I don't know about? You know, so that when you add it into the recipe of your life, things just turn out perfectly? Sometimes I feel like maybe I'm missing some of the ingredients to my *own* life, and the cake just never comes out quite right. Or, like, my life is a box of chocolate cake mix, but the directions to bran muffins got printed on the side by mistake. So no matter how hard I try to follow the directions, I'm never going to end up with chocolate cake, just bran muffins, and should I maybe just be happy and eat the bran muffins and shut up about it? Are you following me? No? Well, that's okay. Sometimes I don't really follow my*self*, either. It's just ... every time I see you, it's like you're the chocolate cake and I'm the bran muffin and all I can think is, "I wish *I* were chocolate cake." Do you ever wish that? That you were a bran muffin? No, I mean, that you had *my* life? Because I sure wish I had *yours*, Sandy. All the time, practically. Ever since we were kids, I always wanted to trade lives with you. I still do. I see you up here with the PTA and the bake sales and the rose bushes and I just think ... maybe I got the wrong directions printed on my box of cake mix. I dunno ... 'Cause I'm out there, slaving away 18 hours a day and nothing feels right. What's the magic ingredient, Sandy? What is it that you seem to have that's missing from the recipe of *my* life?

MAINTAINING APPEARANCES

(Haughty woman who speaks with rolled r's:) Reginald! Come here this instant! *(Pause)* Sit down. *(Then, with a disapproving scowl:) Look* at you ... I'm horrified. Simply horrified. There rarely seems to be an occasion anymore when you don't readily appear to be, well – for lack of a more dignified term – *rumpled.* Frankly, your father and I don't understand you. Your clothing is purchased for you from the finest tailors in London. You have servants galore to wash and iron your apparel, to groom and dress you ... so what could possibly be the problem? For a scion of the Brighton family to go about in such ... disarray? *(Pause)* Well, it will not be tolerated, Reginald. It simply will not. You disgrace this family by not caring about yourself. Your appearance. After all, life is all about maintaining appearances, Reginald. You may as well get used to that cold, hard fact right now. Oh, sit up! For heaven's sake, you're a *man* now, Reginald! *(Pause)* Don't you argue with me, I was taught that a seven-year-old was considered a *man*. So please sit still and tell us which funds you wish to invest in. *(Pause)* No. Don't you *dare*! If you ring for Cosgrove to bring you that blasted etch-a-sketch again, I'll see to it that you're disinherited. You're an adult now, Reginald. Behave like one.

MEATLOAF AND TRUST

(Angry) I didn't ask you to *like* it, y'know! I didn't say you "had" to enjoy my meatloaf! *(Pause; calms herself:)* I was just hoping you'd *try* it. Just try it, Elmer, that's all I'm asking. *(Pause)* No, no, *I* understand ... You "say" you don't eat red meat, fine ... but last week I made that great vegetarian dish, you wouldn't try that either. That thing with the potatoes? Oh, I guess next thing you'll tell me is, it's all a matter of taste. What you're used to. You'll give me that whole song and dance about how some people grow up in the rain forest eating nothing but bugs and worms and centipedes and roaches and so they'd probably find a Denver omelette the most disgusting thing on the face of the earth ... But I want you to know, it hurts my feelings. It does. Because I don't think you have ever once tried anything I've made. Not once! *(Pause)* No, no, you did *not* eat any of the cookies, we gave them away to the guy who lives downstairs! *(Pause)* Or that asparagus casserole either, no, you – *(Pause; a realization dawns on her:)* You're *afraid* of me! You're afraid to eat my cooking! And it's not really the cooking that we're talking about, either. It's not really that at all, is it? It's a Trust Thing, Elmer. A level of trust we're talking about here. Ever since you heard that idiotic drunk detective at the bar implying that my ex-husband died from poisoned food ... you really think I could *do* something like that? Poison somebody? My God! What do I look like to you? A murderer? It's me, Elmer! Me, Vicki! I'm not a murderer! All I want is for you to try the damn meatloaf! That's all!!! *(Pause. Throws her hands up in defeat.)* Okay. Fine. You can't say I didn't at least try. It took me two hours to make this stupid meatloaf, I'll give it to the dog. *(Sarcastic)* Come *watch*, Elmer ... maybe Sparky will keel over dead after he woofs this down!

MOST LIKELY TO SUCCEED

I never dreamed I'd end up like this. Not in a million years. "Most Likely to Succeed." Now look at me: living in a corrugated tin trailer with two screaming brats. *(Yells off:)* SHUTTUP! *(Back to other person:)* A trailer park, Emma! *(Gestures around:)* I'm living in a damn trailer park! *(Shakes her head sadly.)* Everybody warned me about Roy. You ... Momma ... Why didn't I listen? The words "no good" were practically tattooed across his forehead. When y'all said those words, they should've jumped out like warning flags. But I guess when you're in "love," you can't be bothered to listen to reason. You can't be bothered to – *(Yells off:)* I'm not gonna tell you two again! Now shut up!! *(Back to "Emma:")* Now don't get the wrong idea, Emma. I love my life. Really. *(Yells off:)* THIS IS THE LAST TIME I'M GONNA SAY IT!! SHUT UP, OR WE WON'T WALK TO K-MART TOMORROW AND WATCH CARTOONS! *(Back to Emma:)* That usually does the trick. Thank God K-Mart is only two miles away, huh? We can walk over there, sit in the recliners and watch TV. Nobody'll bother us for an hour or so, then they'll ask us to move on. See, Roy sold the TV set so he could buy another gun. As if we need another gun in this place. It looks like an arsenal right now. But it's all right. I mean, at least there's one thing to be grateful for: I'm not *pregnant* again! *(Laughs)* I swear, Roy must have the most aggressive sperm in the country, it penetrates anything. Any birth control is useless against it. So, things could be worse. Right? We could be in one of the *small* trailers. *(Yells off:)* YOU WANNA SLEEP IN THE TRUNK OF THE CAR TONIGHT? THEN SHUTTUP! *(Back to Emma:)* Listen to me ... am I losing my mind? Sitting here like this talking to you, I cannot imagine how on earth I was *ever* considered "Most Likely to Succeed" at anything. That period of my life feels so long ago, and so far away.

MOST MEN

Most men would be happy about this, Stuart. Most men would be doing somersaults, or handsprings, or jumping for joy. Or palpitating. *Most* men would be ecstatic. *Most* men would be overwhelmed with gratitude. But not *you*. Nooooo, all *you* do is grumble and mumble. Grumble, grumble, grumble, mumble, mumble, mumble. See? There you go again: *(Imitates his grumbling and mumbling.)* You've gotten awfully good at grumbling and mumbling, Stuart. *So* good, in fact, that I'll bet you could make a living at it. God knows you can't seem to get work doing anything *else*. Not that I'm complaining. I have always been proud of your talent. Not everyone can paint portraits of the Presidents of the United States on the heads of straight pins. No, I know. I know – Your James Buchanan was called a "veritable masterpiece" by the "Pinhead Press." It's just, well ... there comes a time in every woman's life when this inner alarm clock starts ringing: *(Does the ringing of an alarm.)* Well, that's what it sounds like, in my head ... and I know you're tired – we *all* get "tired," but here we are finally alone together and I am *BEGGING YOU TO HAVE SEX WITH ME! (Pause)* Okay, yes. I admit it: it *is* for selfish reasons. I want a baby! Is that so awful? Does that make me a villain? All you have to worry about – at least for *now*, anyway – is the *sex* part! Don't start thinking about diapers and strollers and college tuition yet. Just think about the sex part! *Most* men would be thrilled! *Most* men would be – *(Apparently, "he" tries to come on to her now, and she becomes suddenly hostile:)* Oh, forget it! I'm not in the *mood* now!

MOTH TO A FLAME

I dunno ... You'd think I'd be smarter than that, wouldn't you? That's what you're saying to yourself. "Isn't she smarter than to go back there and get into this mess all over again?" *(Pause)* I don't know what comes over me ... it's like there's something inside me which *makes* me go back. Like I'm not in control, like it's not me at all, it's this other voice inside my head telling me what to do. *(Pause)* I bet you think I'm crazy. Maybe I am. But all my life, I've had this hunger for guys like Mitch. Guys who would treat me like that. The guys who opened the car door for you, who bought you a corsage – they didn't do anything for me. I was always drawn to the bad boys like a moth to a flame. Bad boys know what women *really* like ... *(Suddenly stops herself:)* Now, y'see? That's that voice inside my head talking again. It's not *me*. Me, I don't want to go down there. But that voice, it's very seductive ... And if I listen long enough, that voice'll lead me down there again, and when I come back, you won't even recognize me. Last time I came back, lips split, bruises all over my body, you remember how awful I looked. Oh, it always starts out all right, but now it's like he's playing with fire and I'm drawn to that fire and it's hard to pull away. I don't want to go down there again, Dana. Just like a moth that's drawn to a flame, if it gets too close it gets singed and dies. I'm not sure if I can stop myself. Help me, Dana. Help me. Don't let me go down there again. Like a moth that gets too close ... I may not make it back this time.

NARROW MINDED

I wish – just *once* – that you would value my opinion, David. But I guess your Mom's right. You're just narrow minded – that's what she told me back before we got married. You see things one way – *your* way – and that's it. *(Pause)* See? Right away, you say "no I don't." Listen to me: Why do you think I'm telling you this? I'm trying to *help* you! What, you think I'm just criticizing you for the sake of criticizing – David, get a grip! You refuse to see anyone's point of view but your own! You get into major arguments with anybody you meet – that guy at the dry cleaners' yesterday about whether or not the coffee stain would come out – who *cares* if it comes out, you don't have to *scream* at the guy about it! *(Pause)* Well ... maybe so. Maybe you *were* right ... *(Wearily)* So then, I guess we're back to square one again ... I see, I see. *(Pause)* David, listen. I'm going to level with you. Your boss called here yesterday. No – David – *listen to me*! I didn't "give you the message" because he wasn't calling for *you*! He was calling for *me*! *(Really trying to get through to him:)* They've noticed what they call a "tendency on your part to be disagreeable." He said they've spoken with you about it, but they haven't seen any improvement. David ... if you don't change, they're going to let you go. They are going to fire you! *(Pause; then, throwing her hands up:)* Okay, fine, then. You really want to lost a great job because you're being a pain in the ass? Listen to me: I will *not* stand here and let you ruin your career just like that. No, I will *not* shut up! I will not shut up until you agree that I am right. Because if you can do that, then – maybe – there's a chance for you. Otherwise, game's over. And you're the one who loses. *(Pause)* Say I'm right, David. Please, just say the words ... "you're right."

NATURAL AFFINITY

Be careful! *You almost sat on Theo! (Pause)* Theo is my prize cat, she's won two blue ribbons and – no, not *there*! Esther is behind you. Esther isn't a show cat, she's just a dear friend who came to live with me after – LOOK OUT! Oh, no! *Now* look what you've done. His *tail*! You've stepped on Archibald's tail! Here, kitty, kitty, kitty. Here, Archie. Poor thing ... *(Indignant)* I do *not*! I do not have too many cats in this house! Perhaps you have too many left *feet*, ever think of that, Donald? You're the only person I know who seems to have a problem with my ca – HOLD IT! Hold it right there ... Don't move! If you move even a fraction of an inch, you'll get sprayed. Cleopatra will spray you. See her? The red one. She hasn't been fixed yet, and ... *(Speaking soothingly to the cat:)* That's a good kitty, Cleopatra, good kitty. It's okay. Good girl. *(Things apparently calm down; then, back to him:)* See what you did? You upset her. *(Offended)* What? They are not "land mines!" They are my pets! My mother always used to say, "never trust anyone who doesn't like animals." She also said, "never trust anybody with two first names." So you have two strikes against you: you hate my kitties, and your name is Donald Craig. Now, you "say" you love me. But as you can see, I have a natural affinity for my cats. So if you want me, be advised that my kitties are part of the bargain. You can't have me without my pets. So what's it going to be? Hmm? And I'd consider my answer very, very carefully if I were you. Because Boris, the most vicious attack cat on the face of this earth, is poised to strike right behind your head, on the mantle. So speak, Donald. What's it going to be?

OCTOPUS LOVE

(Alarmed) Honey? Honey, wake up! WAKE UP!!! *(Relief floods across her face)* Oh, thank God. Thank *God*! I thought maybe you had died in your sleep! You got so *still* ... your eyelids weren't even twitching like they normally do. Yes, they do. When you're asleep they twitch, like this: *(Demonstrates. Then, he asks, "how do you know?")* Oh, because ... I *watch* you. Watch you sleeping. See, sometimes they twitch really fast, like this – *(Demonstrates)* – when I guess you're dreaming, and sometimes they twitch really slow, when I guess you're – what? What do you mean, "shut up and go back to sleep?" That's a nice thing to say – *I was concerned about you*! I mean, there you were, hardly breathing, I thought maybe you had passed on! What would I do? If you died? In the middle of the night – in your *sleep*? What if I woke up and reached over to hold you and you were blue and stiff and cold to the touch? What would I do? Oh, right. Go ahead ... *Yawn*! I'm sorry I'm keeping you up! I can't help it. I love you so much that sometimes I wish I could just wrap myself around you like an octopus and suffocate you with my tentacles. I love you that much. Like an octopus. That's how much I love you. *(Pause)* Oh, don't be *afraid*. I'm not *really* going to suffocate you. I mean it in a very loving way, and all you want to do is go to sleep!

ONCE AND FOR ALL

I don't want to talk about *him*, Beth. No, I want to take just a few minutes and talk about *you. (Pause)* Because. You've levelled some serious accusations against Tony Blakeman, and I just want to make sure – *(Pause)* I am *not!* I am not on "his side." But – listen to me, Beth, because you need to know this: I'm not on *your* side either. I can't afford to take anybody's side. No, the only way I can help you, the only way I can help you navigate through the rocky waters ahead, is to try and stay in the middle. To remain as objective as possible. That's the only way I can help you right now. And the only way you're going to be able to help me help *you* ... is if you give me all the facts. See, Beth, this thing is like a pond. You dropped a rock in it, and now there are some major ripples spreading out across the whole surface of the pond. The only trouble is, the water was a little rough to begin with. *Before* you dropped the rock in. Do you know what I'm talking about? I'm talking about your conduct, Beth. People have said – *(Pause)* No, I'm *not* calling you a liar. That's not what I'm saying at all. It's just that you have a past history of – *(Pause)* Beth, Beth – listen to me! You yell *rape*, and everybody stops whatever they're doing and looks up to see "who did it." You yell *sexual harassment*, and the same thing happens ... only when they look up, they're not just looking at "who did it." They're also looking at "who *claimed* it." Now, you're known around here as somebody who's real hot-to-trot. You've been seen at office parties having a little too much to drink and going just a little bit too far. A lot of people have witnessed what they call "overtly aggressive sexual behavior" on your part. Now all of a sudden you come out and make some very damaging accusations against the Vice-President of this division ... Well, you see the problem, don't you? We've got two, three dozen witnesses who saw you practically making it with him on the xerox machine at the office party last Christmas. But there *were* no witnesses behind his closed doors the other night. Now, I need to know what really went on in that office. And you are going to tell me. The *truth* now, Beth. I want the truth.

NEXT!

PHOBIA

(Recoiling with fear, but also has a case of the sniffles:) Is there any other way we can do this? *(Pause)* Oh. That's what I was afraid of ... No, no, it's not *you.* You're doing a wonderful job, you're very gentle, very kind ... no, it's me. I just have a really strong aversion – *phobia* – to this. Ever since I was a child, when we used to line up in school and get those – oh, you know, for smallpox? The mumps? *Injections.* Yes. *Vaccines* ... Anyway, I would always be the one who fainted. Everything would start to grow all grey and fuzzy around the edges, standing there in line, before I even got all the way up to the school nurse I'd break out in a cold sweat all over, and – boom! Out cold, on the floor. Well, this, this phobia has stayed with me as I've gotten older. *Grown,* right along with me, you might say. Intensified ... it's gotten to the point where – *NO! (Pulls back.)* I'm sorry, I'm sorry, doctor ... I know you think I need that flu shot. But at this point, I think I'd rather live with my sniffles than deal with that needle. No, I know it's not easy to get over the flu ... but it's a lot easier than trying to get over this phobia!

PIG-HEADED

I appreciate it, Miss Watkins, I really do. And I don't mean to sound ungrateful or anything, I mean, this is so generous of you. So very generous. I mean, you were nice to give me this job and everything, but a car!? *(Pause)* No, no, I know it's an *old* car and you're right, you're right, there is a lotta rust ... but I mean, my goodness, it's *still* a – I mean ... *(Pause)* You've always been so kind to us. You always give my mother all those old clothes every spring when you do your "spring cleaning" ... she loves that blue housecoat you gave her year b'fore last, she wears it practically every day I think. And when my granddaddy was in the hospital, y'all sent over that whole great big basket of food – it was so much, I think they're still eating off of it. *(Laughs)* No, no, it hasn't gone bad or anything, lotta that stuff was canned, Spam and stuff like that, it'll probably still be good 'til, like, the year 2080 or something. *(Pause)* My momma always called me pig-headed ... and maybe I am, a little. But sometimes I look at my momma and my granddaddy and all a them and one day it hit me: they've been livin' offa charity alla their lives. It got me to thinkin', it has to stop somewheres. We can't be takin' stuff from other folks all our lives or our kids are gonna end up the same way. So I appreciate your offer, Miss Watkins, I really do. And I hope you won't be offended or anything ... but if you don't mind, I'll let you hang onto this old Buick ... and I'll just keep takin' the bus.

PRICE TAG ON YOUR LIFE

I'm sorry, I get very uncomfortable with bodies in the house ... just don't look at him, okay? Here. I'll move over here ... *(Walks somewhere else.)* ... and you can talk to me. No, face *this* way. *(Indicates, "over here, towards me, not where I was standing before.")* Then you won't have to see him. You know, "out of sight, out of mind?" Okay. Let me just explain ... Jim – *(Gesturing to the floor where she was standing before.)* – is a bum. Not a literal bum ... well, yes. A literal bum. He hurt his pinky finger in a fight on the factory floor two years ago, and he's been collectin' disability ever since. It's the American Dream: all he does is sit in coffee shops picking losing lotto numbers, go out to bars at night and sit over beers picking losing lotto numbers, and then watch TV and see his losing numbers lose. Buying magazine subscriptions to get in the sweepstakes, thinking he's actually going to win the 40 million dollars in prize money. And he's never won a damn thing. Until *today* ... And like the loser he is, he has a heart attack the minute he sees the winning ticket. The only thing he ever did right, and he still managed to ruin it. Now, here's the thing: He's the only person who can claim the forty million dollars. But if he's dead, he can't claim it. Do you understand what I'm saying? Now, I remember two separate occasions when people shouted out to you, "hey! You look exactly like Jimbo Wilson!" And this is the first time I've seen you up close, but I have to admit ... *(Studies him closely:)* You *do*. You really do. So I've got a little proposal for you: what would you say to a new identity? As Jim. *(Indicates where "Jim" lies.)* It won't cost you anything, and you stand to make 20 million dollars, paid out over the rest of your lifetime. Who, Jim? Oh, we'll bury him in the back yard with that cocker spaniel he loved so much. *(Pause)* It's not the worst offer you've ever had. If yesterday, somebody asked you to put a price tag on your life, what would you have said? A million bucks? Two million? I am offering you *twenty million dollars* to forget who you are and be somebody else. C'mon, Doug. You're never going to make twenty million dollars bagging groceries. You'll never even make *half* a million after a whole lifetime of backbreaking work. So what do you say? Are you in with me, or not?

RESPECT

Charlie, I've been pretty straight with you, haven't I? *(Pause)* I think I have ... I've cut you a lot of slack – Charlie, easy. Take it easy. I'm just trying to expla – Charlie, sit down. *Sit down!* *(Pause)* All I'm saying, I've cut you a lot of slack these past six months. You miss a meeting here and there, I don't say anything. But it's my job on the line if they find out, Charlie. Do you realize that? No, I know, I know, you had something you "had to take care of." Well, I've got things I have to take care of too, Charlie, and one of them is you. I'm supposed to be taking care of you! *(Pause)* No, I know you can take care of yourself. You've made that perfectly clear every time we've met. But Charlie, if I don't teach you anything else, there's one thing I want you to get. Because, see, there's one thing you just don't get, and this is what you've got to understand: I *deserve* to be treated with respect. Not just because I'm your parole officer. Because I'm I'm a human being. A person. I've stuck my neck out for you more than once, and – *(Pause)* Okay. That's the way you see it? Fine. We'll do it the way you want. Which means – just so you know, just so we're clear on this: you miss one more meeting, and your ass is grass, Charlie. You miss one more meeting – I'm not finished – you miss one more meeting, I make a phone call and – boom! – you're back in the joint. *(Pause)* Yeah, well, you wanna play this game *your* way, go ahead. Those are the rules.

REVOLUTION

More and more, life seems to be all about waiting in lines. You
wait in line at the bank, you wait in line at the grocery store, you
wait in line at the movie theatre. *(Remembers)* That's funny ... On
the east coast, they say "wait *on* line," and on the west coast they
say "wait *in* line." But no matter how you say it, it's still an
epidemic, as far as I'm concerned. See, in the old days, you had
something known as Free Time. But now, it's all being eaten up
by the time you spend, waiting in lines! I mean, *look* at us. We're
standing here, waiting in line, just to wait in *another line*! My
God! Even on the phone, you call the bank, and you get put on
hold listening to Herb Alpert and the Tijuana Brass for six hours
or something: *(Demonstrates)* Waiting ... *(Hums)* Waiting ...
(Hums) We ought to do something about this. I don't know, start
a revolution or something, refuse to wait in line anymore? I've
never started a revolution in my life, but how hard could it be?
Huh? Overthrow the class that imposes waiting in line on us and
take back our free time! All it takes is commitment. Commitment
and conviction! Well, I'm ready to stand up and say "no more
lines!" *(Starts to rouse those around her:)* You hear that? No more
lines! Let's fight back! *(Leads a chant:)* No more lines! No more
lines! No more – *(Stops, sees something:)* Oh! Wait a minute.
Wait ... *(Notices something:)* The line just moved. *(Gives up the
"revolution":)* Never mind. It's moving now. I don't mind
waiting in line *all* that much after all, I guess ... as long as it's
moving.

RIVER OF LIFE

When? (Pause) Wait, wait, wait ...let me get this straight ... your cat died *two months* ago, and you still haven't *buried him*? I'm almost afraid to ask: Where *is* he? *(Pause. Shakes head, as if to clear it.)* You mean, like, amongst the ice cubes and cut corn and the chicken pot pies? Lying next to the Thanksgiving Turkey ... there's Morris? *(Pause) This* is what I've been talking about. This – well, when was the last time you went *out*? I thought so. Three weeks ... Frank, this is not good. Not good at all. You want to be a hermit? Fine. But I am not going to bear the burden of – yes, you are! You *are* trying to make me feel guilty, trying to manipulate me into feeling sorry for you. Well, I don't. I don't feel the least bit sorry for you. This is exactly what made me leave you in the first place. Your lack of ambition. Of drive ... of taking an interest in anything – except *me*! It's so suffocating, so draining, being the only thing in the world which interests you! You remember when I told you about the river of life? And how it keeps flowing, but it's like you're just standing on the bank, watching leaves and sticks and debris float by? *(Pause)* Okay, look. I came because your landlord called. He was worried. He hasn't seen you in over a month! What were you thinking? That sitting in this hovel and moping was going to bring me back? I'm not coming back. And the sooner you wake up to that, the better. The best thing you can do for yourself is go out and bury the cat. No, not for me. And not for Morris. He's probably freezer-burned by now anyway. For *you*. You're the one who needs it, Frank. You're the one who has to get back in the river of life again. Jump in. Please. For your own good. Before it's too late.

SAD STATE OF AFFAIRS

I was what? I was doing *eighty*? I don't think that's even possible. Because I don't think this car even goes eighty. Maybe your thing is off. Your – you know – your – what d'ya call that? Your gun? Your "speed gun." Yeah. Maybe your "speed gun" is off. Maybe – oh, no! No! Don't open the "book!" You're opening the "book?" You're taking out the *pen*?! Hey. Listen. You can't do this, okay? You can't – Because! One more "moving violation" and I lose my license! *Then* what'm I gonna do? Huh? Okay, okay, look. I've got a valid excuse, all right? *(Pause as she tries to think of one.)* I forgot to set my clock back. *(Pause)* Or ahead, whatever. See, I forgot, and now I gotta be at work, and – *(Pause; surprised:)* How do *you* know so much? Huh? You heard *that*? You heard I got fired? Who told you that? Yeah, well, Mom never could keep a secret longer than five minutes ... Ah, go on, write up the damn ticket. But I tell you one thing, Dale: it's a pretty sad state of affairs, not bein' able to talk your way out of a lousy speedin' ticket, when your own *brother* stops you!

SILENT SURVIVAL

I asked him for a match. That's all. I said, Bill, give me a match. So he reached in his coat pocket and took out a book of matches and handed them to me. That's when I knew. Because when he handed them to me, I looked and it said on there, "Connie's Cozy Kitchen." It had this little picture of a heart in a frying pan. I said, "when did you go to the Cozy Kitchen?" 'Cause, see, McDonald's is usually Jim's idea of a night out on the town. That's the only place we ever go out to anymore, if we even go anyplace at all. He turned all red in the face and said, "I dunno where I got those from. I just got 'em." And that's when I knew. *(Pause)* 'Course, whatever it was that was going on, it stopped. Once I called him on it, it stopped right then and there. I never asked him who she was, or where he met her, or even what they were doing at the Cozy Kitchen! All I know is, pretty soon he got back to bein' his old self again ... *(Pause)* It's a hard thing, living with a secret like that. And we've never talked about it, other than me mentionin' that matchbook that time. And I don't suppose we ever will. I know you like to talk about everything with Andrew, so you probably can't understand this at all, but that's how it is sometimes ... you have to keep some things silent in order to survive.

SPLITTING HAIRS

Are you sure? *(Pause, then confirming:)* You're *sure* about that. *(Pause)* It's just ... well, after it's gone, it's *gone*. Well, at least for awhile, anyway. *(Pause)* Marge, two inches is two inches. Two inches is a *lot*. Two inches is ... let me ask you a question: why are you doing this? I've known you for how long now? All of a sudden, you come in here all worked-up, you "need a change" all of a sudden – why? *(Pause)* No, I'm not trying to pry, Marge. I'm – well, I'm a little insulted that you would even say that. Insulted and, and hurt. Marge, we're friends. Or at least *I* thought so. We always talk about things. Things that matter. Things of substance. How you job is going, how Alan is, my mother – is she dying or is she not dying this week. You know everything there is to know about me. And me about you. Or so I thought. There's more to you and me than just me doing your hair. Hair is just an extension of our inner selves. So you come to me all aflutter, you want me to chop off two inches ... I take that to mean that something is wrong inside. Deep down inside. What's going on, Marge? Is it Alan? Is he cheating on you, and this is your way to lash out? I know there's something going on, Marge. And, sure, okay, I can chop two inches off your hair. But you'll look awful. And not only that, it's not going to solve anything. The only way I can help you – really help you – is if you tell me what's going on.

STRONG ENOUGH

There! Just then! (Pause) You *censored* yourself again! Yes, you did. You *did*! You were just about to tell me what you *really* thought about my singing, and then you stopped and barfed up a big fake compliment instead. *(Pause)* No, it wasn't. It was *not* "beautiful," that's the whole point! I *know* it wasn't beautiful, *I've* got ears! I can hear myself! I sound like a chicken being strangled! So why did you say that it was beautiful? *Everybody* does that to me! They all seem to think I'm not strong enough to hear their true opinion of me or something, I don't know, but they always stop short, just an instant away from telling me what they *really* think, and they *lie*! *(An example:)* Last week, after I gave Bixby that haircut? Bixby. My dog? Anyway, I took him out for a walk, and the vet saw him, and he didn't recognize me *or* Bixby at first and he sort of grimaced – *(Demonstrates the grimace.)* – when he realized what a bad haircut Bixby had, and then he looked up and saw me, and he put on his big fake smile, and he said, "what a lovely haircut, Julia. Perhaps I should hire you down at the animal clinic!" But I could tell he was lying. He was afraid I wasn't strong enough to hear what he really thought of Bixby's haircut. But I am, Milton! I *am* strong! I *am* an adult! You can tell me what you really think! I'm begging you to tell me! I'm strong! I can handle it! Milton, please! If you love me at all, even the least little bit, you'll tell me what you really, honestly think of my singing!!! *(Pause; Milton apparently says something unflattering, and she bursts into sobs:)* Milton! My God! I wasn't *THAT BAD*!!!

THAT KIND OF PERSON

I envy you. No, I do. I really do. Because. You have this, this, I dunno, this ... *knack*, of being perfectly at ease, wherever you go. On the ship ... when we come into port ... in a nice restaurant ... on the beach. All the time. I've been watching you. You are one of those rare individuals who can forget all about your troubles and really live in the moment. At least, that's what it looks like from where I'm standing. And it's been like this flea in my ear, it's eating away at me, wondering what makes us so different? I mean, here we are, we've both put ourselves in hock to take this cruise, but you look completely content about it, and me, it's driving me up a wall! Stress. I'm overcome by stress, my doctor even said, that's why my hair is falling out. Well, you can't tell by looking, but you should see my hair brush. Filled with hair, this big wad of hair, I asked him, "Doctor, why is my hair falling out?" And he said, stress. "Take a vacation." Hah! A vacation ... so here I am, in Greece. I thought a ship would be relaxing. But instead, all I can think about is, how much money this is costing me. I lie awake at night in my cabin, I've divided it up by the hour, even the minute! If I order another carafe of wine, this trip will have cost me $19.21 a minute! If I don't order the wine, it's about a penny less. Isn't that insane? I'm making myself sick, worrying like this. *(Stops herself.)* Oh, listen to me, going on and on and on like this. All I meant was, I really envy you. Because you don't let anything bother you. And I just wish I was that kind of person, that's all.

THREE LITTLE WORDS

I don't have a problem saying "I forgive you," Richard. They're just three little words. The problem is that I'm saying those three little words much too much lately. And all they do is let you off the hook. You tell me you're sorry ... fine. I accept it. But you use those words over and over again as some sort of, of, I dunno, release valve that you can just pull whenever the steam builds up. *(Pause)* You *do*! Whenever your guilt piles up, you need me to say "it's okay." *(Pause)* Well, I've decided something: it's *not* "okay" anymore. I love you, but I will not allow you to walk all over me. *You* have to be the one to take a stand here. *You* have to be the one to decide that you're not going to beg me to say, "it's okay" anymore. And the only way you're going to do that is by living your life in such a way that you don't have to beg for forgiveness every time you turn around. *(Pause)* We're talking about *change*, Richard. Changing your life. Taking responsibility for your actions. I can't do it for you. Nobody can. You're the only one who can do it. Anybody can say "I'm sorry." *(Pause)* I know, I *know* you mean it. But anybody can mean it. What takes guts – what takes character – is to change the way you *live*. So that you don't have to keep saying "I'm sorry" to me. Or to anyone.

TRASH AND TREASURE

Are you going to throw those *out*? *Keep* them! Don't you *know*? Lids off frozen orange juice concentrate make wonderful taps. Taps. You know. Like, for the bottoms of your children's shoes? *(Spies something else:)* Oh, and what's *that*? You can use old pieces of thread like that for dental floss. Really! *(Smiles proudly:)* I guess you haven't lived here long enough to know it yet, but the locals call me "Miss Thrift." On account of, I can use almost anything in a thrifty manner. You know what they say: One person's trash is another's treasure! Why, one summer I made shoes for our children out of some animal cracker boxes. No, no, they were *very* comfortable. I *know* they were. The blisters went away after a few weeks ... and my husband – Ralph – I don't know *what* he'd do without the eyeglasses I ran across in a dumpster! A dumpster! Oh, that's my other nickname, they call me the "Dumpster Diver." Now who in their right mind would throw away perfectly good eyeglasses, I ask you? Prescription glasses! And you know what? They were in mint condition! They're not exactly the *right* prescription, but if Ralph squints really hard, he can make out the signs on the freeway. But the best – the all time BEST – has got to be the wiring! See, we found out that our whole house had to be re-wired, so I scavenged all these old extension cords. Then, together with this old textbook on electricity I dug out of the elementary school trash bin, Ralph did the re-wiring job himself using all of the old cords I had saved. I had miles and miles of those cords. Some were a little frayed ... and, of course, now you can only turn on two appliances at a time without shorting the whole house out – but think of all the *money* we're saving! I guess you could say that thrift is a give-and-take way of life. You give a little, you get a little, you ... *(Eyes widen as if having just seen the Holy Grail:)* Wait a minute! Are you going to throw those out? A perfectly good pair of false teeth? I may need them ... *one* day!

UNSTOPPABLE

I can't believe this guy Jonah. He won't take "no" for an answer. I don't know how to get rid of him, I have tried every excuse in the book, nothing works. First I told him I don't date men at the same office. So he quit. Got himself a great job at another brokerage house, and started calling me up again. So I told him it still wouldn't work, because of the difference in our ages, so he went out and forged his birth certificate! Then I told him that I was sorry, but I just didn't find him attractive. He vanishes for six months, and when he turns up again, I hardly recognized him. He had gone out and had $100,000 worth of plastic surgery done! Oh, yeah, he looks great now, but he's still not the guy for me. So I said, Jonah, I already have a boyfriend. So he hires a private detective to follow me around for three months! Of course I didn't *really* have a boyfriend, but if I'd known I was being tailed, I would've found one real quick – even a fake one – just to stop Jonah. But that's the point: he's unstoppable. So finally I told him – in a moment of sheer desperation, just to get him off my back – I said, "Jonah, it will not work out between us: I'm *gay*!" *(Beat)* No, no, I'm not *really* gay, I just said that. But ... it *worked.* *(Pause)* I *think.* I mean, I haven't seen hide nor hair of him since I told him that. But now I'm worried, see. Like I said, he's literally unstoppable. So what on earth do you think he's up to *now*?

VOICING MY OPINION

(Extremely annoyed by some event which has just happened:) Well, then why did you even bother to *ask*? You only want my opinion if it's the same as yours. Otherwise, it's worthless to you. If I disagree with you – no, you do. You *do*! Every single time, you dismiss me, you – *(Pause)* Like now! Like this! Just two seconds ago you asked me, "Do you want Thai tonight?" And I said, "no, maybe Italian. I don't feel like Thai." And you said, "let's do Thai." Just like that: "let's do Thai." Like I didn't even exist, like my *opinion* does not exist, like I never even opened my mouth to express my opinion! That's just one little example of what you do: how you negate my point of view every time I open my mouth! Why don't you just tell me that the questions you ask are rhetorical, for chrissakes? At least then I won't waste my energy – or my breath – or debase myself by voicing my opinion! *(Pause. Can't believe what she's hearing:)* What? My God! I must be going crazy ... I already *said* I don't want Thai food, so why do you keep insisting that we go to this damn Thai Restaurant? Huh? Am I mute? Are you deaf? Do you hear me? Am I A STONE WALL? DO YOU EVEN ACKNOWLEDGE THAT I EXIST? *(Pause)* What? *(Pause; trying to comprehend some startling news:)* What? What do you mean, a surprise party? For *me*? Oh ... *(Pause)* Well, why didn't you *say* so? In that case, sure, I'll do Thai. Let's go.

WILL YOU STILL LOVE ME ...

I just love seeing older couples together ... Walking along holding hands. Or sometimes you drive by a house and you see them sitting on the front porch together in rocking chairs, just rocking the time away. Sometimes they're even rocking in synch. Rocking in exactly the same rhythm without even knowing it. I just love that. 'Cause you know they've loved each other their whole lives, they've been faithful to each other, and now they can sit back and relax and enjoy each other's company in their Autumn years. *(Pause)* Will you still love me when I'm old? Will you still love me when I get all stooped over and shrink about three inches and my hair turns white and thins out so that you can see right through to my spotted, wrinkled scalp? Will you still love me then? Or when my body is covered with ugly brown age spots from head to toe? Will you still love me? Will you love me when I no longer have my own teeth, and I have to take my dentures out and put them in a glass at night and you forget and drink out of the glass and they're floating in there like big ugly ice cubes? Will you still love me? Will you still love me when my skin draws up tight on my face and around my eye sockets, so that I look like a shrink-wrapped skull? When I become incontinent and you have to change the sheets twice a day? *(Reacts)* Oh, I'm sorry – I don't mean to scare you or anything, I mean I know that's a long way off ... I just want to know you'll still love me.

YARD SALE

All of these are a dollar. *(Pause)* Those? Those are five dollars.
No, I won't budge. No. Absolutely not. I think $5 for a good set
of false teeth is a fair price. They were hardly even used. Well,
let's see ... Dad bought 'em in July, and he choked on that chicken
bone in August ... so he only used 'em for, what? Two, three
weeks? And even then, he only used 'em part time. They said if
only he'd had 'em in that night at Kentucky Fried Chicken ... well,
it's all water under the bridge, now, isn't it? Dad's dead, and now
here's all his things spread out across our front yard with little
price tags on 'em. *(Another person comes up, asks for a price on
another item:)* Two dollars. *(Then, back to the first person:)*
Funny thing about yard sales ... people, they die ... and all their
stuff that was so important to 'em when they was livin' – that you
never paid any attention to – that's all you got left. Like them tools
over there. Dad never did learn how to fix anything ... he always
had to call the handyman after he tried to "fix" the dishwasher or
the hot water heater ... his repairs always made things worse! But
there's his tools ... sitting there, like little reminders. *(Pause.
Almost gets teary-eyed, but fights it:)* Please, I'm sorry – don't try
to talk me down. I know you're just tryin' to save a few dollars.
But they were his, and right now – forgive me for saying so, but it
all just seems a little petty to me.

MONOLOGUES
FOR MEN

NEXT!

ALREADY DEAD

How can you let her *live* like that? Your own *mother* ... What in God's name are you *thinking*, Chris? A storage room, crammed all the way to the ceiling with cobwebs and boxes? No windows ... those florescent lights making everything in there look the same shade of dull, sickly green ... and that *bed*! My God, when was the last time you changed the sheets on that bed? *(Pause)* No, Chris. No, they're *grey*. They *used* to be white, now they're grey. That's how long it's been since you changed the sheets. It's horrifying! *(Pause, then surprised:)* Oh, you think so? You think I'm over-reacting? Well, maybe I am ... maybe to you, she's already dead. Maybe to you, all she is is a big fat life insurance policy, just waiting to pay off. Is that it? *(Pause)* Say whatever you like. But I've caught a glimpse of what you're doing, and it's evil, Chris. It's called lack of compassion. And one day, if there is a God, you will find out for yourself just how it feels to be on the receiving end. You know that saying, "you reap what you sow?" Well, you're sowing it, Chris. And one day you're going to feel just like your mother does now. And I promise you, it won't be a pleasant experience.

BIG PICTURE

At some point, you have to step back and look at the Big Picture and ask yourself, "is this working?" And maybe it is, and that's great. But then again, maybe it's not. Maybe what worked just fine thirty years ago doesn't hold up so well today. *(Pause)* The world is changing, Pop, times are changing, and – no, no. No. I didn't say that. I don't pretend to know the first thing about running a bakery. That's always been your field of expertise, Pop. I just – Pop? Pop! Listen to me – I AM TRYING TO HELP YOU HERE! *(Pause)* I'm sorry. I didn't mean to yell. "Never raise your voice with customers in the store," I remember. That's what you taught us when we were kids. *(Looks around.)* But there's no customers in the store, Pop. That's the whole point. *(Pause; this is hard to say:)* Mom says you've been chipping away at your retirement money to keep this place afloat. And that's very noble, Pop, it really is, but sometimes "noble" don't cut it. *(Very tender, really trying to reach him:)* Pop, I know this place is your life. Always has been. But I *also* know that it's time for you to step back and look at the Big Picture. Look around, Pop. Because from where I'm standing, this place is dying. In fact, if you look around real good, you'll see that it's already dead. I think maybe it's time for you to own up to the fact. And maybe it's time to let go of this place.

BLAZE THE TRAIL

You and your Big Ideas! If I have to eat one more bite of *kelp*, I swear, I'll scream! Or gag. Gag first, and *then* scream. *(Pause)* No, I *know* it doesn't cost anything to raise, will you quit reminding me? Maybe that's why it tastes like I'm eating wet newspapers! *Mold* doesn't cost anything to raise either, but you don't see people lining up to eat *that*, now do you? Honestly ... *(Pause)* Ever since we were kids, Derek, you've always fancied yourself the entrepreneur. And I guess, being the younger sibling, my role has always been to sort of fall behind and play follow the leader. *(Breaks into an imitation of an army-type drill instructor:)* Left, left, left-right-left! *(Stops the imitation:)* Well, that's what it's always *felt* like. Like this private little military academy in our own home, and I was always the lowest rank! Dad has always, you know, been the drill instructor: *(Imitates "Dad":)* "Derek is the brains in this outfit, he'll lead the way, he'll blaze the trail, and you, Martin, you'll back him up!" *(Drops the imitation.)* Well, have you ever stopped to think that maybe I'm tired of always "backing you up?" That one day, maybe *I'd* like to blaze the trail for myself? Try out one of *my* ideas for a change? I mean, if it had been up to *me*, we'd be raising conch down in the Bahamas right now, sitting out in that nice warm sun – not gagging on kelp in Pawtucket in the middle of the coldest winter on record! And in case you haven't noticed, Derek, nobody's *buying* your kelp! We've got ten tons of it and nobody *wants* it! *(Pause)* Yeah, well, maybe I've been marching to your beat too long now, Derek. Way too long. Maybe it's time I went out and found my *own* drum ... and beat the hell out of it for a change.

BLIND

Either this guy is a total idiot, or he's blind as a bat. I mean it! *(Pause)* Remember Jimmy and his whole thing with the smog? Remember? He was all the time going on and on about, "it's burning my eyes! My eyes are burning!" I told him, it doesn't bother me. I told him, if you decide that something's gonna bother you, if you decide something's going to *affect* you in some way – it will. *(Pause)* A coupla years ago my Dad got sick. Really sick. Cancer. Yeah, well, the doctors said it was inoperable and they gave him all these really dire and hopeless predictions. Six months, I dunno, something like that. But you've met my Dad, he's such a fighter, he decided he wasn't going to listen to all that, so he didn't take it in. Plain and simple. He chose to ignore it all, to rise above it. And today he's still out there playing 18 holes of golf almost every day. *(But to get back to the original topic:)* Look, either this guy's a total idiot or he's completely blind – that's so obvious. Don't listen to him. Anybody that would even suggest that you need plastic surgery ... I mean, look at you – you're *beautiful*! Yes you are, you're one of the most beautiful women I've ever known! No, your nose is fine. Look, don't let some stupid guy's bad idea crawl inside your head and take charge. It's only an *idea*. Somebody else's idea. And ideas can't hurt you ... if you decide they won't. You can choose which ones you're going to hang onto, like life preservers ... and which ones you're going to throw away, like garbage. Throw this one away, will you? And come here. I wanna kiss the most beautiful girl in the world.

CHANGE IN THE AIR

(Looks around the room in obvious shock, but trying to contain it:) Well, now. This is ... interesting. Yes, indeed-y. Very interesting. *(Gestures around him:)* Lighting fixtures circa ... what? *(Squints to see better:)* 1977? Hmmm. You don't redecorate very often, do you? Oh, and that stainless steel wet bar ... *definitely* a product of the Disco Era. Well, now. What do I see? I'll tell you what I see: I see a Big Change here. A Change in the Air. A sense of opening up, letting in the light, and doing away with all these hideous accoutrements such as dark wood paneling and – *(Looks down, winces; steps around something on the floor:)* Bear skin rugs. *(His skin crawls; then he pauses and looks closer:)* Correction: *faux* bear skin rugs! *(Looks again still closer:)* Wait a minute ... that's not a bear ... that's not even a *faux* bear ... that's a *dog*! A DOG SKIN RUG? *(Pause)* Well, that's very sweet that you hated to get rid of your pet, but house pets are not recyclable! *(Levelling with his client:)* Look, Mr. David, let me be blunt: your place is in desperate need of a makeover. Now, I believe I can help you. But – and, again, let me be blunt: it's going to cost you. Taste does not come cheaply. *(Avoiding stepping on the rug again:)* Doing away with old dog skin rugs does not come cheaply. *(Pause)* You heard correctly: I *am* the best there is. But you must understand, I'm very partial to my creations. Meaning, if I come back six months from now to check up on you ... there had better not be any dead dog rugs. Or I'm liable to get mad and God knows what. Lose Control. Make a rug out of *you*! Do we understand each other? All right, then. Let the change ... BEGIN!

CLEAN AS YOU GO

What? What is the *problem? (Pause)* All I asked you to do was to wash that pan. Simple enough ... Yet you're behaving as if it's some kind of, I dunno, unnatural act! *(Pause)* There are eggs on the bottom of that pan, Judy! Sticking to the bottom of that pan. Scrambled eggs. But that doesn't bother you, does it? No, I guess it doesn't concern you in the least that the bottom of that pan is coated with scrambled, scorched bird embryos. That they have been adhering to the Teflon for eighteen hours now, becoming *one* with it. *(Pause)* Well, I am sorry if I sound like your mother. But you knew when you married me that I like things clean. Is it wrong to not want to see your soiled underwear strewn about the room? Is it a sin to remove mold and mildew rings from the toilet bowl when they're HALF AN INCH THICK? *(Shakes his head as if to clear it.)* I tried. I tried to wait ... but every time I went in there, I saw that mildew growing and festering and – oh, my God! JUST CLEAN THE PAN! CLEAN THE PAN, PLEASE! I'LL FEEL SO MUCH BETTER IF YOU'LL JUST TAKE THE BRUSH AND SCRUB THAT DAMN PAN UNTIL IT SHINES LIKE IT USED TO EIGHTEEN HOURS AGO!!! *(Pause; composes himself as she cleans the pan.)* Thank you ... thank you. Yes, that's much better. I'm sorry. I guess I just got thrown for a moment. I glanced down and saw that there were no more vacancies in that roach motel over in the corner, and it, well, it *upset* me. But I'll be fine now ... thanks. No, that's good. That looks wonderful. The eggs are all gone, yes. I can sleep now. Sleep ... *(Starts to go, stops, back to audience. Turns around slowly.)* Unless ... *(Pause; forms his question carefully:)* Did you happen to remember to wash the *sheets* like I asked you?

COLD-BLOODED

I don't know. I just couldn't stop. *(Pause)* Now all of a sudden everybody's sayin' stuff like "cold-blooded" and "blinded by hate." Weren't no hate to it 't'all. I'll tell ya what happened. You want me to tell ya, I a l ya: I was drivin' to work in my truck. I was mindin' my own b siness, and in the lane next t'me, there he was, he kept eyeballin' my truck. I leaned out the winda and I said, what you lookin' at, boy? And then he started eyeballin' *me*. So I cut him off at the next stop light, I got outta my truck and he got outta his little shitbox Camero, and he came at me, just swingin' at me. So I started swingin' back. And I hit him and I hit him and finally he stopped movin' ... but I kept right on hittin' him. *(Pause)* Why you keep askin' "what makes somebody do somethin' like that?" I don't know! I just *did* it! *(Because)* He *eyeballed my truck!* And then he eyeballed *me*. I warned him. I said, you better stop eyeballin' me, boy, but he wouldn't. I can't explain it no other way 'cept to say that if I didn't do it, folks'd talk about me. I couldn't let folks talk about me. *(Pause; confused by the question:)* What d'you mean, "remorse?" What the hell does that mean? I killed him, okay? I know I killed him. *(Pause)* No. *(Pause)* No, I don't feel nothing. What am I supposed to feel?

CROSSROADS

Listen, it's not Your Fault. So don't *make* it your fault. The way I see it, ultimately *you* have no say in the matter. The System – the engine, the *machine,* if you prefer – will chug on with or without you, no matter what you decide. So if you're trying to take some big moral stand here, just know right up front that it's not going to make any difference. Believe me. *(Pause)* Look. You got into this business because you wanted to sell. Sometimes we sell goods which are not salutary, which are not good for people, which – Hey, I *know* cigarettes kill! My Dad died from smoking! But it's just an ad campaign you're designing. It's not like you're actually out on the street selling the cigarettes. And even if you were, I still wouldn't blame *you* – like I said, it's the *System*, you have no control over it. *(Pause)* Look, let me just set you straight here: if you pull out on this account, it's not going to make any difference in the world. You think it will, but it won't. Somebody else will step in and take up where you left off. Yeah, well, fine ... You go right ahead and do whatever it is you have to do. Turn in your resignation, if that makes you feel better. Everybody has got to come to terms with their own conscience or their morality, or whatever the hell you wanna call it. As for me, I came to this crossroads a long time ago. I didn't look left, and I didn't look right. I just kept on going. And I've never looked back.

CURVE BALLS

It's funny how things happen sometimes ... You just never know how life is going to turn out. I remember, I used to carry all these napkins and matchbooks and cocktail coasters around in my coat pockets all the time. You know, with little phone numbers scrawled on them. Yeah, well, believe it or not, I used to be quite a ladies' man. Of course, half the time, when I sobered-up in the morning, I couldn't even remember whose numbers they were! *(Laughs; then:)* But this one time ... I woke up one morning and I remembered very clearly meeting this girl at Nick's over on Seventh Avenue ... Couldn't remember her name for the life of me, but I called the number she'd scribbled on one of Nick's little kelly green coasters. Well, there I was talking to her, and it takes me five, ten minutes to realize I've got the *wrong number!* I'm sitting there *talking to the wrong girl!* But there was something *about* her, I just couldn't hang-up ... *(Pause)* You may have guessed by now that the wrong number belonged to Beth. Yep. *(Indicating his wedding ring:)* Five years in July. *(Laughs)* Unbelievable ... *(Laugh subsides:)* You never know how things are going to turn out, Ray. *I* sure learned that lesson. So don't be too eager to outline exactly how you're going to live the rest of your life all at once. Life can throw you some pretty interesting curve balls. But you gotta be ready to catch 'em.

DETERMINATION

Don't ever let me hear you say that again. Nothing is impossible. You hear me? Nothing. When I was out of work a few years back, I got to a point where all I had was nine dollars to my name. I had hit rock bottom. Anyway, my Mom died and I had to get home for the funeral. Now, what do *you* think would've happened if I'd said, "it's impossible?" Huh? I'll tell you what: my Dad would've kicked my butt for not making it back home! So I had my friend Frankie – my only friend in the world at the time – seal me up in a cardboard box and ship me to Wyoming. What I didn't *know* was that Frankie was dyslexic and he wrote the wrong zip code on the box. Six days later – battered and starving – I wound up in Montana. I hitched a ride to the funeral, took me four more days to get there. Only, by the time I finally *got* there, I had missed the funeral by a week and a half! But I made it to Wyoming. Now, *that's* determination. Dad used to say that there were two keys to success in life: one was planning the way you want things to go, and the other is having the determination to get by when nothing turns out the way you'd planned. Well, I've got truckloads of determination, Eileen. So you better get used to that fact right here and now. If I were you, I'd just go ahead and tell me you'll marry me now. Because I will not take "no" for an answer, and I do not give up very easily. See? Planning and Determination. And I've got plenty of both.

DOWN TO THE WIRE

Bob. The crutches? Don't forget the crutches. And tighten your neck thing. Yeah. I mean, what's the point of wearing a neck brace unless you look like you're miserable? There ... that's good. Yeah. And could you moan a little more? Yeah, that's good, that's good ... *(Pause)* Do we need to go over this again? It's not that difficult, Bob. You were rear-ended, your neck is all locked-up, and your bad knee went out. *(Looks down.)* Left or right, Bob. Five minutes ago it was your right knee, Bob, pick one and STICK WITH IT! *(Pause; looks around to see if anyone heard, then:)* Okay. We're going in there, and let me do all the talking. You just remember to moan. Remember, like we practiced? *(Indicates a moan:)* Good. That's very good. *(Starts to go; "Bob" says something which stops him:)* What? Change your – ? You can't change your *mind*, Bob! Not now! We're at the lawyer's office! They're all ready to settle, and all you have to do – *(Someone walks by, and he smiles, pauses, watches them pass, then, with lowered voice:)* Look, Bob. I'm through playing games here. We're down to the wire, and you can't stay on the fence. Either you're in or you're out. If you're in, then let's walk through that door and make a deal with these people so that you can sail off into the sunset with a pile of dough. If you're out ... well, then I guess we don't have much more to say to each other, now do we? What's it gonna be, Bob? In or out? You tell me.

THE EIGHTH DEADLY SIN

What are the Seven Deadly Sins? Let's see if I can even name them all: Murder ... Adultery ... Theft ... Gluttony ... Lying ... How many's that? Six? I can't even name them all. It doesn't matter, though. Because my point wasn't that I could or couldn't name them all. My point is that I've discovered the Eighth Deadly Sin: My sister-in-law, Rhoda. You've seen Rhoda. Yeah. She's some looker. *(Looks around, lowers his voice:)* She works in a strip joint, Bill. Yeah. Can you imagine? When she came to stay with us, I knew right away there was gonna be trouble. She started walkin' around the house with nothin' more than this little towel on. She'd come out of the shower with that towel on and ask me, "have you seen my hair dryer?" Well, now, how the hell would *I* know where her hair dryer was? And then, her towel would start to come loose, and she'd look at me – *(Starts to imitate the "look," then stops himself.)* Well, I can't do it, but you know what I mean. *That* kind of look. Like she's tryin' to start something. Or she'd insist on helping us fix dinner, and we'd be cutting up the stuff for the salad and she'd rub up against me when Susan wasn't looking. Nothing overt, but I got the message. *(Pause)* I don't want to go and tell Susan, because there's already some bad blood between them. And I would never dream of – *(Looks around, lowers his voice again:)* – well, *you* know. I couldn't do that to Susan. Not with her own sister. A few years ago, before Susan, I'd've given my right arm to have this problem. *Now* all I can think is, how the hell do I get her out of the house? Huh? How do I get rid of her, and get things back to normal again?

EYE OF THE BEHOLDER

Whoever said "beauty is in the eye of the beholder" never beheld Bernette! *(Laughs)* Bernette is *so* ugly ... she's practically the ugliest thing on two feet! She's so ugly, she's got to put a paper bag over her head whenever she looks in the mirror! *(Laughs)* No, no, she's so ugly ... well, you get the idea. Bernette is *not* attractive by any stretch of the imagination. *(Laughter subsides.)* But, now, there's another sayin': "looks ain't everything," and whoever it was, said that, got it right. 'Cause what Bernette ain't got in looks, she makes up for in heart. See, she's a woman that's got lots n' lots o' heart, man, I'm tellin' you ... Who else do you know would take the time to feed the – oh, you know, the table scraps to all the mangy stray dogs in the neighborhood? Huh? Would Marissa take the time to do that? No way, man. Bernette, she does that. Lotsa stuff like that. Stuff that makes you know she's a good person. Now, I know Marissa is the kinda woman that gets your blood circulatin'. But lemme ask you this ... let's say you go out lookin' for a woman to marry, who you gonna grab? Some babe like Marissa? Listen: them looks is gonna be gone one day, Jack, and what you gonna be left with then? Huh? I mean, sure, she turns every guy's head when she walks by, but she ain't nice to *nobody*! Not even *you*! See, there's a reason behind that sayin' 'bout beauty bein' "skin deep." Now, see, I *knew* Bernette was ugly from the first time I laid eyes on her, so when I married her, I wasn't ever gonna wake up one day to no big surprises. I mean, you know ... she can't get no *worse*! *(Laughs, then a pause as he becomes thoughtful:)* But – now, I'm bein' serious, man ... I also knew right off the bat that she had a *heart*. Now don't tell me that ain't true 'cause I know it's true. And when you got a heart ... well, it just grows with time. So you think about it real good, man. Don't do like Elmer and wake up one day beside nothin' but a bunch o' wrinkles ... wake up next to somebody that's a good person.

FAMILY TREE

What is it with you? Huh? What is it with this *whole damn family*? You're all crooked, all the way down the line! From the roots of our family tree, starting with great-great-granddaddy Cyrus. He was the biggest crook of 'em all! You've heard the stories about him: legend has it that he painted his little brother up with shoe polish and sold him into slavery on some plantation down South ... and supposedly, then he went and rescued him, and sold him to the same stupid bunch of inbred slave traders all over again! "Anything for a Buck!" That should be our Family Motto. Right up there on our family coat of arms. Let's see ... *(Imagines the coat of arms:)* A knife in someone's back ... a vulture ... and the motto, "Anything for a buck." *(Pause)* If I believed in genes, I'd have to say it's hereditary, 'cause we've all been rotten to the core. But I don't believe in genes, Marvin. I don't believe in heredity, either. And I sure as hell don't believe that I have to live my life the way the rest of you have! *(Pause)* I know, I *know* you're my cousin. But when it comes to what's right and wrong, blood doesn't blur my vision anymore. So you go and find somebody else to cook up your schemes with. I'm not interested.

FAST TRACK

Excuse me ... Do you have any seats left on the flight to Boise? Mm-hm ... Well, how many? *(Pause)* I need to know *how many*. *Because*. I want to *buy* them all! Yes, that's right. *(Pause)* What do you mean, "I can't?" Of *course* I can! You're a ticket agent, your job is to sell tickets, I want to buy *all the tickets left on this flight! (Pause)* No! I'm not a "terrorist," I – listen: my fiancee – excuse me, *ex*-fiancee – let it slip at dinner last night to my boss that I had lied. That I hadn't *really* played football in college, that I made it up because he's a big Steelers fan and I thought it would help me get the job. Well, long story short, it *did* get me the job. So flash forward to today: I got in to work, and all of a sudden I'm the low man on the totem pole. Two accounts suddenly taken away from me, I've been moved from the penthouse to an office in the basement with metal grates on the windows ... in other words, the noose is beginning to tighten. Now, my fiancee – *ex*-fiancee, excuse me – and I are both professional people. We have professional careers. Both on the fast track. Well, I *was*, anyway ... *(Now to the point of the story, with a bit more urgency:)* She is on her way here right now to buy a ticket to Boise, Idaho. She's supposed to be flying to a very important business meeting. If she misses this meeting ... her boss will be furious, and he will begin to tighten her own noose around her own neck. Now, normally I'm a pretty forgiving guy. Normally, I wouldn't let something like this get in the way. But, like I said, I am a professional. And if something damages my reputation, then I am forced to subscribe to the ethic, "an eye for an eye." So ... How many seats are left, and how much will they cost me? I got cash, I got credit cards, I got whatever you need. But I assure you, she is *not getting on this flight!*

GLORY

I never did it for the love of the game. Cobb, Ruth ... they did it because they loved the game. All I did it for was to be noticed. I'm telling you the truth now. To soak up all the attention, to make a pile of money, to get driven around everywhere in limos, to have 16-year-old girls get all hot and excited whenever I made public appearances. To hear the crowd roar when they called my name out into the stadium: "Doug Phillips!" *(Imitates crowd "roar.")* Of course, while all this was going on, I was just taking. I was a pretty selfish, self-centered guy back then. Like I said, I was only ever in it for the glory. Never could be bothered to give anything back. I just took and took ... and so, when my arm finally went last summer, nobody even came around. Nobody called. Nobody cared. No, I'm not feeling sorry for myself, I'm just telling you: nobody gave a damn. I had never given anything to them, never nurtured anything but my own ego ... so there was nobody there to give anything back to me. Who wants to cheer on a loser? A faded star ... a selfish, self-centered prick! *(Pause)* Look, if you don't absolutely love the game, get out. I know from whence I speak. Otherwise, it will eat up your soul.

HAUNTED

What, you don't believe in haunted houses? Well, take a good look around you. Because *this* place is haunted, I can promise you that. Every object in this room is possessed by the spirit of the man who lived here for forty-six years. *(Sees a specific spot:)* Ah ... there's his favorite corner: the *bar*! See all those bottles in there? They'll stay like that from now until eternity. Their levels never dipping any lower. Forever half-full. Or I guess he'd say half-empty. Doesn't matter now. *(Pause)* I guess it sounds like I'm talking crazy, eh? Well, I don't know about you, but *I* sure can feel it. My father's presence, on every doorknob, on every chair, on every window sill, covering every square inch of this place like a tenacious, invisible layer of dust you can't wipe off. If only you could know the oppression he created in these rooms. And I'm not talking about myself now – I left when I was seventeen. I'm talking about my Mom ... my sisters ... he ruled this place like a titan while he was alive. I'd shrink three inches when I walked through this doorway and he was waiting for me. But now he's only a memory. *(Pause)* I'd forgotten just how small these rooms were. When you're a kid, they seem gigantic. The funny thing is, even though he's dead and gone ... this clinging sense of fear way in the back of my head still remains. Isn't that funny? Everything else is gone. He's gone. She's gone ... in a few days, weeks maybe, all this stuff will be cleared out and the house itself will be gone ... but that sense of fear and dread still remains. Tangible. Just like all this crap he's left behind. When I pick up his favorite shot glass, when I sit in his favorite chair ... I *feel* him. Wrapped around me, like an old familiar coat you forgot you had squirreled away in the back of your closet. *(Pause)* I feel him, Marie. So don't tell me there's no such thing as a haunted house. My memories are the ghosts, and I'm standing amongst them.

HIGH TIME

Riff never picks up the check. You go somewhere, just you and Riff, he don't pick up the tab, you go three, four people, he *still* don't pick up the tab. He don't ever pay his share. He don't even *offer*. I don't know what it is with him, he seems to think he's entitled or something. *(Pause)* It's always something – either he left his wallet at home or he forgot to go by the bank – you just watch. It's always something. Well, today he's gonna learn his lesson. 'Cause, see, we're all going over to the Chinese place for lunch. And we're all gonna say we forgot our wallets. I already talked to Fong – he's the fella who runs the place – and Fong's gonna pitch a fit, he's gonna insist that Riff go back in the kitchen and wash dishes. But the thing is, he's gonna be bringing Riff the dirtiest, grossest dishes you have ever seen. I got that big stew pot, we left it in the backyard last summer, it's coated with grime, I brought it in, Fong is gonna scream at Riff until he scrubs it clean. And then, just when Riff thinks he's all through, Fong is gonna say, "now you gotta wash my car." By now, the rest of us will have left – well, not really, we'll be hiding in the back, watching. And you just wait 'til you see Riff's face when he takes a look at Fong's *car* ... It's a 4-wheel-drive, Fong took it out into the woods last week after that big rain. It's got about two inches of crusty mud all over it. *Covered* in mud. Fong is gonna hand Riff this little bitty worn out old sponge and a bucket of tepid water and say, "when it shine, you can go." Man, I can't *wait* to see the look on Riff's face! *(Pause)* Oh, don't be such a softie. Riff is a mooch. And it's high time he learned his lesson.

JUNK TALKER

Oh, no. He's looking over here! Quick, pretend we're in the middle of a very serious conversation. Because! It's *Bob! (Pause)* What, you don't know about Bob? Oooh ... Well, let me tell you: *(Motions for the ou.. son to come closer, then whispers:)* Bob is a – how would I put ? – a possessive conversationalist. Yeah. He gets ahold of you – well *me*, I should say, I'm his "favorite" at the moment – he gets ahold of you, and he won't stop talking! And it's not like a conversation, there's no give and take. It's just this big, long monologue. Anything that flies into his head, he's like a sewage tank of idle conversation. Not that his talk is dirty or ugly or anything ... it's just meaningless. It's junk. You know, like getting junk mail? Eating junk food? Well, Bob is a Junk Talker. And, like I said, see, he dominates. Boy, does he dominate. You can't even get a word in edgewise! That's why I would really appreciate it if you would pretend that we're engaged in a very serious, meaningful – oh, crap! Here he comes! Please, quick, if you could just – *(Sees "Bob" and smiles a big fake smile.)* Hi, Bob. Well, we were just – *(Apparently, "Bob" has started talking, and won't stop.)* Yeah ... ? *(Long pause.)* Yeah, I – *(Interminable pause. Really play this pause as long as you possible can, reacting to Bob's babbling the whole time. The longer you play the pause, the funnier it will be.)* Yeah, that's – *(Another doozy. Finally, you interrupt "Bob:")* Bob, I have to go to the bathroom. Would you exc – ? What? You do *too*? Yeah. *(Wearily:)* Yeah, we can "talk" on the way. *(Exit)*

KEY TO SURVIVAL

Robert Crestman. That's my name: Bob Crestman. *(Pause)* Except in Texas. In Texas, I'm Bob Longhorn. And in Maryland, I'm Bob King, and in Wyoming, I'm Bob Miller. Oh, and in Vegas, I'm ... what *am* I in Vegas? *(Laughs)* Oh, yeah. Bill Silver. I got so many Drivers Licenses, I gotta carry 'em all around in a suitcase! *(Laughs, then stops abruptly:)* That was a joke. I don't *really* carry 'em around in a suitcase. I carry 'em around here ... *(Indicates his head.)* In my head. That's why I can't accept your kind offer of a drink, boy, 'cause I gotta keep my mind straight. I gotta know who I am, and where I am, at all times. Why am I tellin' you all this? Because you sit there thinkin' this is some kinda game. Well, it's *not*. There are all kinds of variables that you haven't even considered. Things you have to think about. Things you have to keep straight. All the time. Who are you? *(Pause)* I don't mean your name, stupid, I mean who *are* you? Why do you wanna do this? Because, I'm telling you: in this game, you got to know what you're doing and *why* you're doing it. *(Rolls his eyes:)* I am *not* being "hard on you." Trust me: if you get into this with me and you get caught, the cops are gonna be a *lot* harder on you than I am right now. They are gonna bust your balls, mister. So don't play big bad grown-up tough guy with me. I'm telling you like it is. *(Pause. Then, softer and a bit repentant:)* I know I haven't given you much. I haven't had much *to* give you. All right, let's lay our cards on the table. I've been a lousy father. But now I'm ready to give you this, if you want it. But you can't be coming here, saying you want this because – what? You want to "get to know me" or you want to "get close to me." That's a load of bull. This is a serious game, and if you want to play, you'll be playing with the big boys, and you got to know who you are at all times. *(Pause)* Good. Just so we understand each other. I can't play "father" to you. I got too many other identities I gotta keep straight. One more will break the camel's back. *(Pause)* Second thought, I *will* have that drink. Then I'm gonna tell you what you need to know in order to survive out here. I guess I'm not a bad father after all, eh? How many fathers can hand their sons the key to survival?

LAND OF PLENTY

(This speech is played as if standing at a deli counter:) Ah, listen, Can I ... can I *owe* you the dime? *(Pause; then, desperate and humiliated:)* Because, I don't ha – okay, wait a minute, *wait just a minute* ... *(Frantically searches his pockets.)* Look, I'll pay you the difference. I *will*! I just don't have it on me right now. I can give you the rest – *no*! Don't take it back! What good's it gonna do you? You gonna try and sell it again? A lousy half a pound of bologna? You son of a – ! How many times have you waited on me? Huh? And now you won't trust me for a lousy ten cents? *(Pause)* Okay. Okay, I'm sorry, I ... *(Looking around the store, calming everyone:)* I'm sorry, everybody. I'm okay, everything's okay now, all right? *(Back to the original person, very humble now:)* Look. I'm sleeping in a damn cardboard box down by the river. A cardboard box, man. I used to have a penthouse apartment, and now look at me. *(Levelling with the deli counter person:)* All I want is somethin' to eat. I'll find a couple bottles, I'll find change on the sidewalk, I'll get you your ten cents, but will you please give me a break? Please? Just think if you were in my shoes right now. You'd want somebody to do the same for you. *(Apparently the deli person relents.)* Thank you. Thank you very much. I promise, I'll pay you back.

LEDGE

(Standing on a building ledge many stories up:) Don't look down, Charlie. Okay? It's just me, Charlie, I told 'em I wanted to come up here all by myself, it's okay. It's all right. Just don't look down. *(Pause. He glances "down," then:)* They called out two engine companies for you, Charlie. Two whole engine companies, and half the 15th Precinct is down there too. *(Pause. He looks around, feels a cold night chill, then:)* God, it's cold up here. You cold up here? *(No response.)* Hey, you 'member that time he hadda go up on the 125th Street bridge? Yeah, you do. It was so cold that night ... I just about froze my nuts off, standin' out there with the wind whippin' through those guide wires, 45 miles an hour, you remember? It was makin' this howlin' noise, that wind whippin' through those wires? I think it was, some kinda record cold, I dunno, you remember? You tried to talk that guy down. *(Pause)* You remember his wife, Charlie? When we hadda go over there, tell his wife? You remember that? He wouldn't listen to you, and you remember we hadda go over and tell her, and she was cryin' her eyes out – okay, okay! *Don't!* I'll stop. I'll stop. Watch me. I'll shut up. I'm shuttin' up, now, Charlie. I'm shuttin' up. *(Pause)* Y'know, it's not the end of the world, Charlie. It's not. Guys – lotta guys – have been on the "take" before, lot of 'em have gotten caught, y'know, it blows over. Eventually, it all blows over and you go on. Life goes on. *(Pause)* No, I know. I know ... you probably are gonna lose your badge. But you're not gonna lose Arlene. You're not gonna lose me. We're here for you, Charlie, and we're not goin' noplace just because you felt you hadda – you know. That don't matter to me, and I know it don't matter to her. *(Pause. Then, very gently and sincere:)* Come on down, Charlie. Please. I can't go over to your place and tell Arlene that you ... *(Pause)* I can't do that, Charlie. I can't. And I don't think, deep down inside, that you want me to have to. *(Reaching out with his hand, slowly:)* Come on in off this ledge with me, Charlie. Come on down. And I promise ... I'll help you sort all this out. We'll sort it all out. Together.

LEGACY

What do you want me to say, Pop? That I want you to come live with us? *(Pause)* Well, I'm sorry, but that's how it is. All my life, growing up, you were always too falling-down drunk to give a damn about me. Never knew where I was, or what I was off doing. You couldn't be bothered. Fine. So I grew up alone. I grew up without a father. *(Pause)* I don't want your pity, or anybody else's pity. That's just how it was, and never – not *once* – did I ever feel sorry for myself, not one day in my life. But now you want me to feel sorry for *you*. Now, all of a sudden, I'm supposed to throw my life away, give up everything I've worked for for the last twenty years, and take care of you. Pop, I won't do it. You hear me? I will not do it. Michelle says it's unhealthy for me to carry around all this anger towards you, and it probably is. It's probably going to eat my insides out one of these days, but I don't care. You hear me? All I've ever felt towards you is anger. All you've ever given me is hate. That's your legacy. So don't expect me to throw my arms out all of a sudden and welcome you into my home. There is no welcome mat out for you, no red carpet. You were only successful in one thing, your whole life. And you wanna know what that was? Turning my heart into stone. That's all it feels like in here, is a big block of stone. So live with that, old man. I've got my own life to live.

NEXT!

LIGHTEN UP

Will you *please* calm down? It's only a fingernail! People break fingernails every minute of the day, they don't have a *fit* about it. *(Pause)* Yes, you did, you *did* have a fit! Well, personally I would classify a "fit" as your eyes bulging out and you screaming louder than the fire alarm. Which is exactly what – correct me if I'm wrong – you just did. *(Suddenly hears something:)* Wait a minute ... is that somebody at the door? Look at that, you woke the next-door neighbor up! See? I *told* you it was a fit! *(Calling off, towards the "door:")* No, Mrs. Kramer, everything's fine. No, we – No. It's – We just broke a fingernail. *(Pause. "Mrs. Kramer" is apparently incredulous.)* That's right ... a *fingernail.* I'm sorry. I – Mrs. Kramer, I'm sorry we woke you up. Go back to – go back to ... good*night!* *(Pause, then back to the original person:)* Y'see that? You woke up Mrs. Kramer! Now that definitely classifies as a fit, because she sleeps sounder than a mummy! *(The whole point:)* This is what I've been telling you. These "fits" you have all the time. You're like a little kid, throwing a tantrum. Over the slightest thing. You've got to lighten up, Daniele. You've just got to. I worry about you. I really do. Because if you're going to flip out and have a fit over something like *this* ... what are you gonna do when the *baby* comes, huh? Have a coronary? Yeah, well, just in case you've forgotten, you're going to have a baby in about four months! Yeah, well, you'd better learn to lighten up before the baby comes, or I don't know what's going to happen. Because – listen to me, it's reality-check time here: you're gonna have baby food being slung all over the kitchen ... in your hair ... a child screaming when you're trying to talk on the phone ... yeah, well, you *better* think about it. Because it's going to be your crash course in Learning to Lighten Up. Because with a kid here, you are either gonna be forced to lighten up, or you'll just implode from having a fit to end all fits. Trust me: I'd rather not watch you implode. So let's start now ... take a deep breath ... *(Does so, leading the other person:)* Let it out ... *(Does so again:)* ... and lighten *up* a little.

LISTEN TO MOE

Moe called. And he said to do it. He said, "go 'head." That's what Moe said. So if you say you wanna do what Moe says, then we gotta go. Now. *(Pause)* Hey, it's not up to *me*, see. If it was up to me, I'd say no. I'd say "*hell*, no!" But it's not up to me. Moe's the guy, see. If Moe says go, then you go. If Moe says not to go, then you'd better *not* go – if you know what's good for you! *(Pause)* A lotta my time is taken up, sittin' around here, waitin' to hear from Moe. *(Pause)* Or Erasmus. Only ... Erasmus don't call no more, now that I think of it. He tells Moe to do all the callin', and then Moe calls and says where to go and what to do. *(Pause)* It's not such a bad setup we got here. We got us a warm room in the winter. Cool room in the summer. And all the beer you can drink! Hah! *(Laughs, then laughter subsides. Pause)* Okay, so we gotta go out and get a little tough sometimes. Rough some guy up or somethin', he's behind in his – you know – his payments. That's the tradeoff. Look, it's not up to me. If it was up to me – *(Catches himself, stops.)* Well, it's *not* up to me. That's the whole point. What I think don't matter. It's all up to Moe. All I know is to listen to Moe. And Moe said we should go, so let's go. *(Pause)* Jimmy? Jimmy, what're you waitin' for? He said to go. Don't go gettin' a conscience on me now. It's either them, or you. What's it gonna be?

LONG STORY SHORT

Well, to make a long story short, I went down there. Went down to talk to the guy. The – yeah. I says, I need some more a those two-inch nails, and he says we ain't got no more two-inch nails right now, and so I says you had 'em yesterday. So he says, lemme go in the back and check. *(Pause)* Well, to make a long story short, he's back there for, like, half an hour. Twenty minutes. Whatever. I go back there and he's sittin' here drinkin' a grape Nehi and eatin' some peanuts. The salted kind. Or maybe roasted. I can't remember now ... anyway, long story short, he says, you can't come back here, can't you read that sign? And he points to a sign that says, "Employees Only." And I says to him, where the hell are my two-inch nails? And he says he hasn't looked for 'em yet. I says what the hell you been doin', sittin' here on your duff drinkin' a grape Nehi? And he says, "yeah. Do you mind?" Well, long story short, I *did* mind, and I says to him, if you don't get me them two-inch nails, the only way you're gonna be drinkin' that damn grape Nehi is intravenously. *(Pause)* I dunno, it's amazin' when you get into a situation like that what comes outta yer mouth. Yeah. A guy like me, sayin' somethin' like that! Hah! Well, long story short, I finally got my two-inch nails. *(Pause)* How? Well, that's a *long story ...*

LOUSY OUTDOORSMAN

This is it! This is the last straw! I mean it, Jackie – the last time I ever let you talk me into one of your famous "weekend getaways." I *knew* it. The minute you mentioned the word "camping." I knew that this was going to be just another in your long line of big ideas that I was not cut out for. You want some six foot five strapping muscle-bound guy in a lumberjack shirt – that's not me. And it'll never *be* me, no matter how many outhouses I try to sit in, or how many cords of firewood I try to chop. *(Examines his palm:)* I've still got those callouses ... *(Then, back to the subject at hand:)* Jackie, let's face facts: I am a lousy outdoorsman. I set fire to our tent with the sterno can. I dropped my car keys into that pit toilet. And now, a bear has eaten my wallet. Swallowed. All of my credit cards. All of my cash. The very idea that I, Peter J. Callahan, am crawling around in poison ivy – as you just pointed out, thank you very much – to wait for this 1,200 pound creature to do his *business* so that we can then dig through his fresh, steaming feces *with our bare hands* to recover my Optima Card ... I just can't keep it up, Jackie. I can't keep trying. When I try to be an outdoorsman, I fail. Every time. You want a lumberjack? Go find one. If you want me ... *(Turns attention elsewhere:)* Uh-oh. I think he just went. Tails you go, heads I go. *(Flips a coin; then, visibly very disappointed:)* Damn! Two outta three? You see what I mean – I'm a lousy outdoorsman!

MORONIC MONIKERS

"Manheim?" What, are you *serious*? "Manheim" ... That's not a name, that's a *country*, I think. Or a city in Eastern Europe or someplace, I don't know. But whatever it is, it's not a name for our son – or a daughter. *Especially* not a daughter. *(Pause) What?* "Gladys?" What *century* was that book printed in, anyway? Huh? "Gladys" is not a name for a little girl growing up in 20th Century America. No, it's not. It's a name you hear shouted across bingo cards on Tuesday afternoons at the Senior Citizens' Center. Or, or, heard whispered with raspy voices in the dark corridors of convalescent homes. It's an old ladies' name: "Gladys." *(Pause)* What? "Seven?" What, are you seriously suggesting the number 7 for a child's *name*? Oh, "Sven." Sorry. Well, not unless he's blonde and Swedish and six feet tall and he's got 200 pounds of muscle. He sure as hell isn't going to get that from you, and in case you haven't noticed, he's not going to get it from me, either. *(Pause)* Yes, I am, I am, I'm *very* serious about this. But the names you keep coming up with are atrocious. They're atrocities. What do you mean, like what? Like, all of them! Yesterday you called me up at work to ask me, what did I think of Aristotle? I said, "I think he was a great man. Oh! You mean for a *name* ... !" Aristotle? C'mon! Or, or, we're in the car last week, and you start reading street signs out loud! Oak! Forest! Elm! Main! I am not naming our child Main! I'm just not. *(Pause)* Honey, I'm – no, I'm not. I'm not! I am not criticizing your sense of adventure. I love your sense of adventure. But when it comes to naming a child ... no, it's not that I want something "boring," like Joe or Bill or Bob or Sue. I agree with you, being different is good, I just don't want something which comes out sounding oddball for the sake of being different. Okay? So, we have an understanding now? *(He smiles. A warm, gentle moment.)* Good. You were beginning to scare me with all these moronic monikers, they ... *(Pause)* What? You're not serious. "Moniker?" Oh, my God! I think I'm going to *scream*!

MY CANVASS

I like it. I like working all day long with people who don't talk back and don't give me any lip. *(Pause)* I *know* they're dead! Hah! That's why they don't talk *back*! Look, every job has its tradeoffs. That's a fact. I know this is a little hard for you to understand, but I'm an artist, and I've learned to look at them as ... my canvass. A very unusual canvass to be sure, but my job – as I see it – is to create a masterpiece on whatever canvass I'm given. Look, I know this must sound totally morbid to you, but it's the only way I can get through the day. If I stopped and looked at them as dead bodies, I'd go crazy. But you get used to it after awhile. Believe it or not, you even get to a point where you can actually *joke* about it. I remember this one time they brought Chuck Higgins in here. You remember Chuck Higgins? Yeah, well, he was the big bully back when we were in 7th grade or whatever. I remember, he used to beat me up every day at recess. So, anyway, Chuck goes out and kills himself drunk driving, and they bring him in to me. And I get this irresistible urge ... to do Chuck in drag. I put a wig on his head ... lipstick ... a dress on him ... the whole works. Because I knew that if Chuck were alive he'd *die*, because this is the last way Chuck Higgins would want to be seen. *(Pause)* No, closed casket. So Chuck's ten feet under even as we speak, wearing a string of pearls, a really nice Halston dress, and high heels. *(Pause)* This is all I'm saying: you think you'll never get used to your new job. But you will. I mean, hey. If I can adjust to dead bodies ... you can certainly adjust to tax audits!

MY OWN WAY

Nope. Sorry ... but no thanks. I wouldn't drink a cup of Earl Grey if it were the only tea bag left on the face of this earth! *(Pause)* Chamomile, mint, orange citrus, Lemon Zinger ... I've tried just about every kind of tea there is. They don't do anything for me. You know how I always was growing up, I always sort of found my own way of doing things. I guess I finally decided that I needed my own kind of tea, too. I actually discovered it by accident, thanks to Skiddy. Remember Skiddy? My cat? Yeah, well, we had this package of catnip one time, and Skiddy was playing with it, and he dropped it into my mug of hot water one morning. I was barely awake, I thought it was *tea*. But I'll tell you: one sit of that catnip ... *(Takes a deep breath, exhales.)* ... and I felt invigorated! Hah! *(Begins to lick the back of his hands. Note: He will never comment on his odd behavior in this piece, but keep talking calmly and normally while doing the specific actions.)* It really bugs some people. Christine actually moved out, it freaked her out so. "How can you drink catnip?" she asked me, "it's like, *pot for cats!*" I said, what's the big deal, it's just an *herb*. She thought it was so bizarre, I never told her I spiked her birthday cake with it. You know, that carrot cake I made her last year? *(Starts to wipe behind his ears with the back of his wet hand like a cat.)* It was all in her head, she actually claimed that I was *behaving* weird after I started drinking catnip tea, isn't that absurd? I read this clinical study on catnip, some medical journal, I don't know, it only affects cats. Not humans. Something to do with the brain synapses or whatever, I don't know, but it is completely ineffective to humans. *(Begins to lick in between his fingers very intently, as if cleaning claws.)* The funny thing is, I've never really liked cats. But I feel a really strong affinity for this catnip tea. It's not like Ginseng, see, because the really incredible thing is that it wakes you up in the morning, and puts you to sleep at night. Not like caffeine. And not – *(Begins to hack and cough as if coughing up a fur ball. Take a long time with this, and do it as realistically as possible. Then, when you're finally finished, resume talking calmly as if you've never started.)* Hey. You want to go out and get something to eat? I've had this incredible craving lately for fresh seafood. *(Lets out a big meow.)* What? You're looking at me funny. You're looking at me like Christine used to. I swear! Sometimes I think you're all going crazy.

NICKNAME

"What's it *mean*?" You wanna know what it *means*? *(Laughs, looks around to a "group" of others who are apparently standing around:)* He wants to know what his new nickname means! *(Laughs with them, then turns his attention back to the first person to whom he was speaking:)* Well, as you know, the Boss always wants something that rhymes. Scary Larry ... Bob the Slob ... So he took *your* name: Rick. And he added the first part. *(Pause)* You're still not seeing this, are you? All right ... do you remember last Tuesday when you were on the elevator and me and the Boss got on? You remember that? Okay. Well, do you remember what you were doing at the time? Well, then, I'll refresh your memory: you were picking your nose. Yeah, that's right. In front of the Boss. Well, the Boss hates it when people pick their nose right in front of him. It shows a lack of respect, he says. I mean, that's the natural conclusion *I* would come to. If somebody was pickin' his nose while I was talkin' to him, I would consider it a less than respectful act. Oh, but you didn't just pick, Rick. You *flicked*. The Boss offered his hand – despite the fact that your finger was buried up your nose – the Boss was willing to look past that. Forgive it. Cast it out of his mind. And shake the hand that had been probing for boogers just moments before. *(Pause)* But, *at that critical moment,* you *flicked.* To take his hand, you had to flick off your little prize. And, unfortunately for you, your flick landed on the Boss's lapel. Maybe you didn't notice it. But he did. And he said to me, "who the hell was that?" And I said, "that's Rick." And he said, "who?" Cause he can't hear so good any more. And I said, "Rick!" And he said, "Pick and Flick Rick." So, you see, you have to be careful what you do in public ... you never know who's going to see you. *(Pause)* So that's how you got your new name, Rick. And I hate to tell you, but I got a feeling you're gonna be stuck with it for a long, long time.

NO-WIN SITUATION

Look through *Cliff's Notes* ... you'll see. All the great novelists have always relied on their imaginations. I mean, *c'mon*! Did Herman Melville *really* go out and battle a giant whale before he could write about it? No! *He made it up!* Was Charles Dickens *really* visited in the middle of the night by three ghosts and taught the true meaning of Christmas? Or for that matter, was there actually a Grinch who *stole* Christmas? No! It's *literature*, Danny. These were all the products of somebody's imagination. Which brings me to *my* little ... situation. I wrote this book, see. A non-fiction book. Well, it's classified as non-fiction – but it's really fiction, if you know what I mean. *(With difficulty:)* It's called ... "1001 Ways to Make Your Woman Squirm with Ecstasy in Bed." It's sort of a How-To manual. But the thing is, I've never actually *done* any of the things in the book! I just made 'em all *up*! Fantasized about 'em all, wrote 'em all down one day ... and then, just as a joke, I gave it to my editor friend, Laura. Yeah, well, she *flipped* over it! Offered me two hundred thou right on the spot to *publish* it. How could I say no? *But.* The thing is ... when Susan finds out about this – Susan, my *wife*? See, she thinks she's the only woman I've ever *been* with! And she *is*! But she's gonna take one look at this book and think either: (a) I lied to her about being a virgin and I'm more experienced than I ever let on; (b) she's gonna be pissed-off that I've never tried any of these exciting techniques out on *her*; or (c) she's gonna think I've been cheating on her ever since we've been married! It's a no-win situation, Danny. No-win. I should've ignored my literary yearnings and never written this thing in the first place, but like Herman Melville, I followed the whale. But the whale's leadin' me upstream, Danny, and I don't know what I'm gonna do once I get there. How in the world am I gonna tell Susan about this book?

OPERATORS LIKE ME

(Seductive) You have the most outstanding earlobes I have ever seen. So *delicate* ... like little rose petals, puckering, just begging me to nibble on them. To caress them with my tongue, to – Olivia! Don't back away! You invited me up here to – I'm what? I am *not*! An "operator?" Olivia! I am being totally sincere with you! Every word out of my mouth tonight, I swear! *(Pause)* I *know* its been ten years, but that's what high school reunions are for, aren't they? To rekindle old flames? Sparks? You remember those sparks we used to make? Like striking matches in the dark. No, I haven't had too much to drink, now come here. *(Apparently, she does. His demeanor becomes seductive again:)* You have the most outstanding earlobes I have ever seen. So *delicate* ... like little rose petals, puckering, just begging me to – what? *(Then, in shock:)* What do you mean, I already *said* that? *("Olivia" apparently takes a swing at him, because he ducks.)* Olivia! *(Trying to recover:)* It was *not* a "line," I was being totally sincere! I – *(Some unbelievable piece of information is dropped like a bomb.)* WHAT? She said – WHAT? Well, she's a liar! I have never, ever used the Earlobe Line bef – I mean – *(He realizes he's caught. Pause. He runs out of steam, seems to deflate before our eyes.)* Okay. All right ... you got me. You win. It *was* a "line." But it is my *best* line, all right? I want you to know, at least I saved my best line for you. *(He laughs.)* My God, will you listen to me? I guess some things never *do* change, do they? I guess I still am a bit of an operator. *(Pause; he becomes very genuine, very sincere – a big change comes over him:)* But I *do* miss "operating" with you, Olivia. I mean that. The biggest mistake I ever made was letting you go. And that is not a line. That ... for the first time in my life, I think, is the truth. So, if you'd like, I'll be happy to drive you home now. No tricks. No strings attached. See? Even an operator like me can have a good heart sometimes.

PAIN

I know I caused you a lotta pain, Eloise. I know that. That's why I laid that hoe out against the pig pen fence over there'n. I want you to pick it up ... go on. That's it. Now: I want you to hit me with it, as hard as you can. Eloise – listen to me! I was awful to you, and I know I hurt you. And that hurts *me* inside. Hurts so bad, I feel like I ate ground-up glass. But I want us to get past that. That's why I'm reformin'. I'm in the midst of reform. I got up early, milked all the cows, collected all the eggs, and now it's come to me that I got to let you hurt me in a very physical way. *(Pause)* I know it won't make a difference, but I want you to know that Sheralee didn't mean nothin' to me. I think it mighta been her waitressin' costume that got to me, that's all. That short little skirt she was wearin' an' all ... well, anyway, it was just a one-time thing, and I didn't really enjoy it. I was worryin' about *you* the whole time. Look, I know I hurt you, and I want you to get even with me. So you hit me as many times as you want with that there hoe. I'd much rather you do that than go out and cheat on me just t'get even. *(Pause)* I aim to prove to you that I'm sorry. Really and truly sorry. And if gettin' whacked with a hoe is my own humble way of showin' ya ... well, then by God I'm ready. *(Braces for the worst.)*

PROBLEMS

Lemme tell you something: you think *you've* got problems? Believe me, this nonsense you're sittin' there drownin' your sorrows over is *nothing*. But never mind what *I* think ... My job is to listen. I know that's some age-old cliche or something, but I'm not supposed to burden you with *my* problems. You're supposed to burden *me*. I'm the bartender, it's my role. Only thing is: you're not burdenin'! The dog chewed up your shoes? Big deal! You dented the car? So what! *(Pointing to the drink:)* You want another? Well, drink up, for cryin' out loud, you sip like a little old lady. *(Pause)* Problems ... Hah! You ain't got problems. You wanna hear problems? Okay, *I'll* tell you a problem. I'll tell you a king-sized problem – *(Stops himself.)* – only ... I *can't*. I'm supposed to let *you* confide in *me*. *(Pause; apparently the customer insists.)* You really wanna? You really wanna hear? Okay: *(Leans in confidentially:)* I killed a guy. There. I've said it. *(Pause)* Oh, there's *more* ... See, the cops are closin' *in* on me! It wasn't even my fault, see, that's the thing. Some creep tried to mug me, and I slugged him. Then I kinda slugged him again and again until ... well. You get the picture. Then the cops come along after I'm gone – yeah, I left – and find out this guy is a businessman. They decide it's a homicide. Decide he was, I dunno, askin' me "for directions?" Who knows. But, see, *I* know better. I know he tried to mug me. *Why?* Who *knows* why. His wife is sick, he hates the world? Who cares "why?" All I know is, they got an "eyewitness" and it's only a matter of time before they haul me outta here in handcuffs and ... *(Pause)* Yeah, well, you asked me what my problem was, now you know. Now you know! So drink up ... All of a sudden, your problems don't look so bad anymore, do they?

PROSPERITY

Your what? Your *lips* hurt? *(Pause)* No. No, I am not calling an ambulance because your lips hurt. It's just – no! It's out of the question! If the ambulance people will even come *up* here anymore. God forbid you should *really* get hurt and need help. Because, Gloria! You call 911 for any and everything. It's like crying wolf, only you're crying ... I dunno what. Lips. Crying Lips. Last week, it was your nostril. Do you have any idea how humiliating it is for me to call 911 and tell them my wife's nostril is on fire? Excuse me. "Aflame." Yes, "aflame" was the word you used. I don't know how that tamale got up there either, but just because we live in a 12-bedroom home does not give us the liberty to abuse the city's rescue forces. Yes, yes we do pay taxes. But that does not entitle us – you're not listening to me – we can't – Gloria! *Get a grip! (Pause. Composes himself.)* Y'know, I think "wealth" is the worst thing that ever happened to us. "Prosperity." Back when we were poor ... I mean, look at you: nowadays you're stuck in this big place all day long without anything to do. That's why you sit around thinking about your lips hurting and your nostrils burning and your eyelids falling off. *(Pause)* Okay, then *peeling* off, whatever. Remember back before we had all this money and leisure time? You used to get out there and *work*. Okay, volunteer work, but you used to think about people besides yourself. But now, you sit in here, isolated all day, with nothing to think about but what body part you want nipped or tucked by Dr. Wiedman. *(Pause)* Well, I'm sorry, but that's what you get for waking me at four a.m. to tell me your lips hurt. Your lips are fine, okay? Now go back to bed, and – *(His eyes widen.)* Uh-oh. Wait a minute. Ow! Oh my God ... it's my *toenails*! They're aching again. Now see what you've done? You've got *me* started! It's contagious, Gloria. Complaining about one body part gets somebody else started before you can say – OW! Quick. Call 911, will you? This is serious! Tell them – *OW!!!* Tell them my toenails are *throbbing uncontrollably!*

PROVE YOURSELF

They used to have a name they called me. "Momma's Boy." I grew up without a father around. Just Momma and my four sisters. So I guess maybe I did come off a little effeminate at times. And it didn't help that my sisters used to dress me up in their dresses – I was the baby, see – and parade me around the neighborhood. I didn't know any better, I was only a toddler. But people remembered it. The kids in the neighborhood, I mean. And it became this, this "thing" that I had to overcome as I got older. *(Recalling someone yelling at him:)* "Hey, Momma's Boy." I used to pick fights just to prove that I was really a man. Fights with big guys too, lotta times I got creamed. It was like I had to prove myself everywhere: in the classroom, on the playground ... I went out for every sport there was. Track, basketball, baseball ... I wasn't big enough for the football team, I remember, I ate six meals a day for four months trying to put on weight. I had to weigh, I dunno, like 160 or something was their minimum weight. I had stuffed about 8 or 9 burgers down my throat right before tryouts and I weighed exactly 160 pounds. So I get down there for tryouts and I'm all ready to kick ass. I'm primed. I'm pumped. I'm ready to go. Only ... I had stuffed my face so much that the burgers came up. Right there on the field. But I played awesomely, and they were still gonna take me, too, only when they put me on the scale again, I came in at 156 after tossing all those burgers. So they wouldn't take me. I went out and beat some poor kid up that night, I was so mad. *(Pause)* Listen, Greg. Don't do like me. Don't feel you have to "prove yourself." You have something that nobody else in the world has – you're you. That's what makes you special. So just be yourself. You'll be a lot happier that way, I can promise you that. Take it from one who knows.

.

SCENT OF FEAR

(Quietly menacing:) Man, I can smell it on you ... it's all *over* you,
like cigarette smoke. *(Pause, then:) Boo! (Laughs)* Lookit you,
man! Lookit you jump! You know what that is? That's fear. You
gonna have to get on top a that fear, or you ain't never gonna
make it. What you thinkin', anyway? Huh? You think we need
your help? What you think we "need?" You come down here, you
gonna – what? You gonna "help clean up the ghetto?" You gonna
teach me some gansta motha how to "talk nice?" Talk like *you*?
What's that gonna get me? Huh? I'll tell you what it gonna get me,
it gonna get me killed. See, you don't know, man. You don't
know how it *is*. I get mixed-up in this, helpin' you ... they liable to
turn on *me*. *(Pause. Then, really trying to communicate:)* You
come around for a couple days ... a week ... you think you gonna
change things. You ain't gonna change nothin'. Ever'body still
gonna be carryin', and they still gonna be shootin' each other and
that's just how it is. Why? I dunno why. 'Cause somebody's
standin' on somebody else's corner. Or, somebody looked at
somebody else's woman. It don't matter "why." Don't waste your
breath talkin' 'bout "why." That's just how it is, man. You can't
even understand. That's why, if you want to do anything here, you
got to get that fear outta yourself first. 'Cause that's the first thing
they gonna smell. And if they smell it ... it's all over.

SILVER STUD

(Elderly man:) You got anybody in here that wants some good lovin'? Well, I'm ready! I *been* good an' ready since 1971. That's the year Maybelle passed on, bless her heart. Right before she went, she told me, she said, "Carl, you find somebody else. You still got a lotta spark left in your sparkler." So if anybody around here's got a match, well, then I'm ready to sparkle. I'm whatcha call yer Silver Stud. They kicked me out of Sunset Gardens. Said I was too "rambunctious." But I ain't rambunctious. I'm just lookin' for love. That ain't a bad thing, I don't think. It just takes energy. And drive. And I got both. Now, I know you got "qualifications" here. And I'll do whatever I need to in order to "qualify." But I can't promise I won't let my spark plugs spark. I can't swear I won't let my "tilt" light light up. *(Pause. Becomes agitated:)* Listen to me. Listen! You can't tell *me* what I can and can't do! I – *(Pause; composes himself, then, very humbly:)* All right. I'll level with you: I ain't got nowheres else to go. You heard a them babies they deposit on peoples' doorsteps in baskets? Orphan babies? Well, I'm an Orphan Dad. My son ain't around no more, he got hisself killed overseas, and ... well, you gotta take me. I ain't got nowheres else to go. I know I talk big sometimes about my spark plugs and what-not, but it's only talk. You can let an old man talk a little bit, can't you? Can't you let an old man talk? What's it gonna hurt if I need to think a myself as a Silver Stud? It don't hurt nobody to think that things aren't as bad as they seem.

SLIP OF THE TONGUE

I said *what*? I did not call the Boss's wife *"fat!"* *(Pause)* I *did*? I said that? You mean, to her *face*? Oh my God ... I don't even remember ... *(Pause)* I mean, I have always thought she was pretty large. All right, *huge*. And a woman her age, the way she stuffs herself into those little black leather mini-skirts – *(Shudders at the thought.)* But I would never call her "fat" to her face. *(Pause)* Really? Gosh ... well, what did she say? Uh-huh ... Well, thank God for small miracles. I mean, that her hearing aid was turned down. *(Reminds him of a broader idea:)* Y'know, it's weird, but I have these thoughts – I guess we all do – all flying around in my subconscious all day long, and I wish there was one day when you could tell everybody exactly what you thought of them and not be held responsible. *(Suddenly blurted out:)* I wish you didn't always have to be so damn "right" all the time. *(Pause)* What? I did not! I said ... what? *(Pause)* "... damn right all the time?" My God ... is this, like, Teret's Syndrome? I've started walking around in a daze, spewing forth truths to the world? *(Pause)* Well, they *are* true, Allison. Everything I've said here tonight. *Truisms.* The fact that the Boss's wife is fat and that you always have to be right. *(Pause)* No, no, I didn't *mean* to say it, it just popped out! *(Blurted out:)* Well, I wish I had *never married you in the first place* – *(Grabs his mouth.)* I didn't mean to say that! No, no, that wasn't another "truism." That was just a slip of the tongue! I promise! I don't know where all these "statements" are coming from all of a sudden, maybe it's all the anxiety from waiting to hear about the promotion or something, I don't know ... but I swear, I have never for one moment regretted marrying you. Ever. *(Pause. Waits to see if anything else is going to "pop out." Calms.)* There. See? Everything's fine now. *(Quickly covers his mouth to prevent another "truism" from popping out.)*

STONED

(Staring dazed, straight ahead.) Hey, man. I dunno, I – *what?* What's that, dude? My *name? (Pause, he thinks hard for a moment, then starts to giggle.)* I think I forgot! *(Pause)* Wait a minute, wait a minute, let's see ... gosh. What *do* I remember? I remember taking a hit off this *really* strong joint. Alfonso brought it back from Mozambique or some weird place. And then ... well, I was ... and they ... but ... wait. But ... no, I was ... I'm ... ooh, boy, this is hard. Kinda like wakin' up in the morning, only ... is it morning, or what? Okay, now. What if ... no. Okay, okay. Let's say ... but what does that have to do with my name? What does that have to do with the price of eggs? *(Pause)* What does that mean, anyway? "What does that have to do with the price of eggs?" Do you know what that means? *(Pause)* What? My name? *(Pause, he thinks, then starts to giggle again.)* Oh, man. I think I forgot all over again. Only, I don't know if I ever remembered so that I could remember before I forgot. Does that make any sense? Am I making sense? That's what happens when you get stoned sometimes, man. You don't make any sense at all. *(Shakes his head, as if to clear it.)* I shouldn't have smoked that joint. Alfonso warned me. He said ... *(Stops, thinks.)* What did he say? *(Tries to remember, then:)* Well, whatever he said, I didn't believe him. And now look where I am! *(Stops, looks around, puzzled:)* Hey, man ... where *am* I?

STRIKE

What do you mean? *(Pause; looks around him.)* You mean, just shut it down and leave? Let me get this straight: You're asking everybody here to – no, no I heard what you *said*. I just wanna be clear about a few things. Like, when are we coming *back*? *(Pause)* Hey, I'm not worried about a "wage hike." I'm paying my bills *now*. What I'm worried about is walking out on this job and not having a job to come back to. That's what I'm worried about. And, for what? *(Pause)* Look: all I know how to do is work this lathe. That's all my father knew how to do. He taught me, on this exact same spot where we're standing right now, how to make hand-crafted legs for chairs and coffee tables. Now maybe I'm wrong, but I don't think that I can just walk out on the street and find another job like this. It's easy for you to say, "everybody has to go on strike." But it's not some game. Not to us, anyway. It's not like we're playing some kids' game and somebody's gonna yell "olley olley oxen free" and it's all over. No, this is real life here, mister. You're talking about taking food out of people's mouths. People I know. People I love. People I work with. *(Pause)* No, I'm not tryin' to be a troublemaker. I just want to know exactly what to expect ... and I'm gonna hold you to it. Because this is my life we're talking about. My life, and everybody else who works here.

TALK TO DAD

Billy, can I talk to you for a second? Come here. I gotta ask you something. It's gonna sound kinda funny ... *(Pause)* Are you afraid of Dad? I dunno, I guess that sounds sort of silly, doesn't it? I mean, we're all grown up now and here we are, home from college and everything ... But you gotta admit, he does have a temper on him. *(Pause)* But you never were scared of him, were you? Like that time when you and me snuck into his liquor cabinet and we, you know, we drank that, that whole bottle of creme de mint or whatever it was. Because we liked Junior Mints so much, remember, we thought it was a drink that would taste just like Junior Mints. And we got really really sick at the stomach and I guess we were drunk and we took mom's lipstick and drew all over the walls ... I don't know what we were thinking. He was fit to be tied when he got home. I was so scared. But I remember, you marched right up to him – you marched right up to him and you said, "daddy, if you didn't want us in there you should've put a padlock on it!" Thirteen years old! *And he backed down!* From a thirteen year old! You stood up to him and he backed down! *(Takes a deep breath, then:)* Well, it's like this: last night, see I – I borrowed dad's car. No, well, I sort of didn't *ask* him, exactly. After he went to bed I borrowed his car and I, ah ... I wrapped it around a tree out on Mission Road. Yeah, and it was his '57 T-Bird. His prized possession. Yeah. Look, I know it's Christmas morning and everyone's going to be coming downstairs any minute to open the presents and everything but that's why I need you to talk to him for me. Before he finds out. I don't want you to take the blame or anything, no, nothing like that – just would you please talk to him for me? I hate to ask you to do this, but I know if *you* were to talk to him, he wouldn't get mad. And the last thing I need right now ... is for him to get mad.

TOUGH LOVE

She asked me, how much do I love her? I said, well ... a lot. That's
how it all started, see. I said I loved her a lot. So she said, would you
walk a mile for me? I said, okay. She said, barefooted? I said, well,
sure. She said, all right, how 'bout would you crawl a mile on *broken
glass* for me? Now ... I hadda stop and think about *that.* I mean, I'm
not the smartest guy in the world, but do know better than to say
somethin' stupid right off the cuff. So I thought for a minute and I
said, how 'bout *half* a mile? But she started tearin' up like she was
gonna cry again, so I said, okay, okay, a *mile*! And then she looked at
me with them piercin' green eyes and she said ... "then *do* it." Just like
that. "Do it." Now, I thought she was just kiddin' around, so I started
to laugh. But she wasn't laughin' back. *(Pause)* That night, I wake up
in the middle of the night. There was this awful racket out in the
garage. So I go out there, and it's her. I say what the hell are you
doing? She said, crushin' up all these old Coke bottles. She's crushin'
'em up and shovelin' all this crushed-up glass into the back of my El
Dorado. Now, this is what I would suppose you might call "tough
love." I heard them talkin' about it on *Oprah* or one of them things
one day. Provin' how big your love is by how tough you are. Or
somethin' like that, I wasn't really watchin', it was just on in the
background. But the point is ... what is the point? Oh, yeah. She said
– and *all she said* – was, "when it gets light." And then she went off
to sleep. Now, she's gonna wake up in about – *(Checks his watch.)* –
half an hour, and she's gonna start that car. She's gonna ask me to get
in. All I can imagine is that she's takin' me out somewheres and she's
gonna dump all that glass out on the ground and tell me, start
crawlin'. To prove I love her. Now, I *do* love her. Really, I do. I love
her so much, I'm tempted to get down on that glass and crawl. But
this got me to thinkin', surely, *one* of us is insane. I mean, come on!
Now, I'm sorry to wake you up in the middle of the night like this,
Eliot, and frankly, I apologize. But you always been a good neighbor
... a reasonable sorta guy. And I know you're a psychiatrist ... so what
I wanna know is, which one of us is crazy? Her or me? If it's me, then,
well, I'll just go on and crawl on that glass, cause I really do love her.
But if it's *her* ... well, you see what I mean? I'm gonna need to get her
some help. And I mean *fast.* Before she wakes up and tells me to start
crawlin'!

TRAFFIC JAM

(Seated, gesturing ahead with tremendous frustration:) Look at this. Will you *look* at this? We're not even moving. I'll bet this traffic's backed up ... five, six miles. If only you didn't have to go back to get your sunglasses. If you hadn't gone back to get your sunglasses, then I wouldn't have had to run that red light, and we wouldn't have had to stop and get that ticket. And if we hadn't stopped to get the ticket, I wouldn't have insulted the highway patrolman and we wouldn't have had to sit there for ten minutes and listen to his lecture! If only you didn't have to go back to get your sunglasses ... *(Pause)* And a donut. If only we hadn't stopped to get you that cruller. If we hadn't stopped to get that cruller, then I wouldn't have gotten stuck talking to that guy from the homeowners' association. If only you hadn't stopped to get that damned cruller ... *(Pause)* Or the umbrella. You were so afraid it was gonna rain, we just had to pull over at the side of the road and buy an umbrella from that guy sellin' 'em on the street. And now look — it's as sunny as it can be! Not a cloud in the sky. If only you hadn't stopped to get that umbrella ... *(Pause) Me*? Don't blame *me*! *You* were the one who had to stop for the sunglasses and the donut and the umbrella! *(Pause)* Well, so *what* if I got up half an hour late? It's not *my* fault! If only you hadn't wanted all that stuff, we wouldn't be stuck here in a traffic jam right now!

TURNING INTO OUR PARENTS

Oh my God! Did you hear what you just said? Of course you heard it, you *said* it! You just asked him, "if Joel Johnson jumped in a fire, would *you* jump in a fire?" That's something your *mother* would've said! Don't you see? *We're turning into our parents!!* *(Pause)* I *knew* that something was going on ... I could feel it. Some, some transformation taking place deep inside me ... the things I've begun to do. Like turning the answering machine off whenever we go away so that I don't have to return any long distance calls ... Or turning the heat down to 56 degrees all the time. Bobby complains that he's freezing to death and all I say is, "put a sweater on." *Just like my father!* Or some of the things I've heard *you* say. Echoes of your mother's idiotic little remarks ... like, "what if your face froze like that?" Or, "sticks and stones can break my bones ..." What? You don't think that's idiotic? *Everybody* thinks their parents are idiotic! It's a fact of life! I used to swear that, one day, when I had kids, I would be so "cool." I would be so "in touch." Well, I'm *not* in touch, and it scares me! I'm turning into my father! Do I *look* like him yet? Is my hair going? It's going, isn't it? And I'll bet I'm getting a paunch around the middle, too. This is just like a horror movie! Like the werewolf. Only it's not a werewolf I'm turning into, it's my father, it's George Clark Sr., from Great Falls, Idaho! *(As if caught in the "throes" of a werewolf transformation:)* Ahhh! Ahhhh! *(Anxiously pleading to the unseen other person:)* Help me! Please help me! Tell me I'm not turning into George! Tell me! *(Pause)* I'm *not*? Are you *sure*? *(Takes a moment, calms himself.)* Whew. That's a relief. I just wasn't ready for polyester sport shirts and sans-a-belt slacks quite yet.

WHISTLING PAST THE GRAVEYARD

Yeah, well, I'm sorry, maybe it *is* funny ... but I'd rather not joke about it, if you don't mind. See, when I was a kid – *(Glancing up at a second person who is passing by:)* Hey, get that over to ballistics, will you? *(Back to the original person:)* What was I saying? Oh. When I was a kid, my Grandmother used to say to me, "don't go whistlin' past the graveyard." She had all these superstitions, you see, and one of them was that if you passed somebody's grave in a, well, let's say a carefree manner, that you were somehow bringing it on yourself to be the next one lying in that cemetery. *(Glancing up at yet another person passing by:)* Oh, hey, is there any more coffee? Thanks. *(Back to the original person again:)* Yeah, boy, it's cold out here. Coldest day of the year, I heard on the news. *(Pause)* She never would've understood standing out here in the freezing rain ... sleet ... poking around a dead body, digging 9mm shells out of the mud, cracking jokes about what an ugly son of a bitch this guy is. *Was.* Not that I'm superstitious or anything. I'm not saying, because I crack a joke about this guy, that *I'm* gonna get run over by a dump truck tomorrow. It's just ... *(Composes his thoughts, then:)* After awhile you see so much of this. Out on the streets like this? So much senseless killing. So much needless violence. And your heart gets so heavy ... I just can't joke about it anymore. I just can't.

WORST JOB IN THE WORLD

You think you've got it bad? Just imagine what it's like sticking your hands in people's mouths all day long. Scraping plaque off their teeth, poking into their diseased gums with metal instruments hour after hour, eight hours a day, five days a week ... what? Oh, no, no, *I'm* not a dentist. Whatever gave you *that* idea? Hah! No, I was just *saying* ... selling real estate is not the worst job in the world. *(Pause)* No, see, *you* said "selling real estate is the worst job in the world," I was simply disagreeing with you. Coaching a paraplegic soccer team would be up there too. Or a blind frisbee champion? Now, *those* are hard jobs. But, c'mon. How hard is it to sell a house, for cryin' out loud? You just unlock the door, let people in, and say "wanna make an offer?" I could do that in my sleep! *(Pause)* See, we all gotta learn to be more grateful for what we have. Most of us spend half our time bellyachin' about what we *don't* have, when what we oughtta be doin' is spendin' that same time bein' grateful for what we *do* have. *(Pause)* Okay, so you hate your job. I say, that's life. Listen – you oughtta try wrestling alligators for a living sometime. Now *that's* a hard job. I oughtta know ... that's what *I* do. No, I'm serious! *(Gestures down.)* Them fancy shoes you're wearin'? They was probably made outta one a my adversaries! So don't talk to me about the "worst job in the world." Them alligators have got the worst job of all. I mean, at the end of the day, at least *you* don't have to worry about windin' up as somebody's billfold!

WRONG MATCH

(Talking through a big, fake smile:) How's this? *(Poses silently for a moment with the smile, as if a picture is being taken, then, still talking through clenched, smiling teeth:)* What's the matter? No, no, when the little light comes on, the flash is warmed up. Then you take the picture. Okay, okay ... *(Back to a big, fake smile again.)* Wait. Now you've got your finger over the lens. *(The other person apparently removes the finger.)* Good. *(Another thought:)* Oh, what number is it on? The number. What number – look on the bottom. *(Pause)* What? There's *got* to be a number on it, if there's no number then that means – *(Smile vanishes.)* My God, Darlene! You forgot to buy FILM? Here we are with our toes touching the Pacific Ocean – the most spectacular sunset I have ever seen in my life, right behind us – and you're telling me you forgot to buy *film?* *(Suddenly explodes:)* I WANT A DIVORCE! I know, I know, we've only been married for – *(Looks at watch.)* – twelve hours, but it's so clear to me now. We're the wrong match. It's obvious: the inside of my car is neat and tidy and yours looks like a pig pen. I'm frugal and I keep track of every dime we spend, and your bank statement comes back with nine or ten bounced checks every month! It's wrong, Darlene! Can't you see? Us – this whole match – it's all terribly, terribly wrong, and now – what? *(Pause)* You do? *(He forgets his anger and melts in affection for her:)* Oh, I love you too, Darlene ... here. *(Gets ready for photo again:)* I know there's no film. We'll just pretend. *(Another big smile, this one genuine:)* Cheese!

ZIPPY WHITEHEAD

I can't stand Zippy Whitehead. This is all his fault! *(Pause)* Jealous? No, I'm not! Not anymore. Not anymore, now that – well, maybe I am still a *little* jealous ... but if I am, it's for all the right reasons. You see, all the time, growing up, Zippy Whitehead was the spoiled rich kid in town. He had everything handed to him on a sliver platter. Everything his heart could want. He had all the best toys, he had his own sandbox, his own treehouse, his very own swing set! And if that wasn't enough, he had his own swimming pool! Olympic-sized swimming pool! For a 10-year-old boy! Then, when we got to high school, he had a Jaguar. Not the animal, Ted. The *car*. One day I took out my Boy Scout knife and I scraped the corkscrew thing all the way down the side of Zippy Whitehead's black Jaguar. The scratch must've been a quarter of an inch deep, that corkscrew just sunk right into Zippy's fresh paint job like a hot steak knife through a stick of butter. I hid in the bushes and watched. I just knew Zippy would have a fit ... but he *didn't*! His dad got the car repainted, and Zippy had it back in three days! This went on for years, me trying to find a way to upset Zippy Whitehead. I couldn't get into Harvard like he did – I couldn't afford it. I couldn't get a job in one of the Top 5 Wall Street brokerage houses like Zippy Whitehead did – I didn't have the right "connections." I was consumed, I lost sleep at night from this desire to find some way to get the best of Zippy Whitehead. Something that would really eat away at him like he had eaten away at me all my life. Then it hit me: *Susan*. So I stole his girlfriend away from him. His fiancee! I thought, "this is how I'll show Zippy Whitehead! I'll steal his *girl*!" So I set out to work on Susan. I charmed her. I wined and dined her. And now ... there she is, in there, waiting for me at the alter, and the upshot of it all is that Zippy Whitehead couldn't care less! I'm marrying this woman that I can't stand just to get even with Zippy Whitehead, and he doesn't even care!! He's never cared about anything, his whole life, and now ... *(Gestures around him, as if to say "now look.".)* Yes, yes, I guess I'd better go in now ... they're playing The Wedding March. Look, Ted. Don't ever let your jealousy run away with you like it did with me. Learn a lesson from the guy who spent his whole life trying to get the best of Zippy Whitehead, eh? Jealousy does not pay.

APPENDIX:

GUIDELINES FOR A SUCCESSFUL AUDITION

1. **Pick the right piece.**

    For general use, select a piece which represents who *you* are. You should always have a monologue ready to perform at the drop of a hat, an introductory piece of work (a "calling card," if you will) which gives auditors some idea of who you are and what qualities you possess – both as a person and an actor.

    On the other hand, if you're auditioning for a specific character – a character very different from yourself – then select a piece which showcases qualities which are similar to that particular character. For example, if you're up for the role of a "dopey surfer-dude" type, you might go in with a monologue like *Stoned* (found in the "Men" section of this book).

2. **Be specific.**

    As you begin working on a new piece, take the time to figure out to whom you're talking and what your objective is. In all of these pieces, the characters are pursuing an objective of some kind, and I hope that, in most (if not all) cases these objectives are fairly easy to identify. Remember: none of these characters are talking simply for the sake of talking! They're all speaking to one (or more) specific person(s), and trying to get something from that person (or persons). So make sure you know specifically (the more specific the better) to whom it is you're speaking, and exactly what it is you want from them. It's always more interesting to watch an actor *going for something specific*, rather than just standing there talking without a clear objective.

3. **Pick a piece that's the appropriate length.**

    If you know that you've got a two-minute slot, pick a piece that's a little bit less than two minutes long so that you can take your time and play moments and pauses. Don't try to stuff a three-minute piece into a two-minute slot. I've spoken with auditors who frequent the S.E.T.C. (Southeastern Theatre Conference) auditions, in which actors are given 60 seconds to audition. The auditors' biggest complaint is that the actors pick two-minute pieces and try to say them as fast as they can – in other words, "cram" them into the 60-second slot. Time and time again, whenever someone gets up there with, say, a 45-second piece, takes their time (which, I'm told, is *not* often!) and plays the pauses in the piece, the auditors stop, look up and pay attention!

4.   **As the character, try to play a change or transition during the piece.**

I try to provide at *least* one (sometimes more) built-in transitions in many of these pieces, so that the auditors can see you play different qualities. For example, if you start out angry, during the piece you might calm yourself and really try to reason with the person to whom you are speaking. Or if you start out laughing, you may, as the piece goes on, grasp the gravity of the situation and become serious. As an actor, you can use your imagination to create an "arc" in each monologue you prepare – in other words, show a change in the character's thinking, going from point A to point B. Or, better yet, from point A to point B *to point C!*

5.   **Don't resort to "shock value" simply for its own sake.**

Using overtly crude language, disgusting gestures and shockingly sexual images or phrases *solely to get the attention of the auditors* usually backfires, leaving you with mud on your face.

6.   **Listen.**

If the auditors give you some directions and ask you to try the piece again with those directions, *listen to what they are telling you* and give it a try their way. If you don't understand, ask them to repeat or rephrase their directions. If you need a little more time to think through the piece again, ask if you can have a few minutes. I know it can be scary to throw out all your preconceived ideas and perform your piece again differently, but there's no reason to be afraid – all they're trying to do is see how well you take direction, and how easy you are to work with. Above all, *don't be argumentative* with the auditors if you don't agree with their direction. You have nothing to lose by trying it their way, and everything to gain – your willingness to give it a try might even get you the job!

7. **Have a few remarks prepared.**

Auditors sometimes ask you to "tell us a little something about yourself." Think about this beforehand and always have some remarks ready, so that you're not stuck up there going "ah ... uh ... well ..."

8. **After the audition is over – *forget about it!***

It's over. Let it go. Don't spend the rest of the day (or the *week*, for that matter) worrying about what you did or didn't do, should've said but didn't say. Sometimes those who give the worst auditions end up getting the job, and those who give the best auditions never get a callback. That's life. Do your best, then leave it behind and move on.

9. **Remember: they want to like you!**

Actors become insecure and nervous when they go into an audition, they're afraid they "won't be liked." Rest assured that when you walk into the room, the auditors *want to like you.* They want you to be great – hey, it makes their job easier if you're the one for the job – then they're done! So just try to relax and have a good time. Remember, auditioning is very subjective: if you were to audition for a panel of five individuals, each one of them would probably have a completely different opinion about your work. Oftentimes, who does or doesn't get hired has little to do with you yourself, so remember – don't take it personally. If they're casting a drama and they've already got a leading lady who's 5' 10" and you come in to read and you're a guy who's 5' 5" and you give the most brilliant audition in the world ... well, you probably won't get that particular role because most likely they're looking for a guy 5' 11" or taller. That's just how it is sometimes.

10. If the auditors introduce themselves, take them in.

You know what I mean. Look them directly in the eye and shake their hands. In my own experience behind the audition table, if I notice that the actor is too frightened to make eye contact when introduced to me, or too afraid to even look at me, I become instantly worried about them, and it makes me very nervous to watch their audition. If it's obvious that they don't feel secure about themselves, then I don't either – I become afraid *for* them.

11. Two words about resumes: don't lie.

It's an old cliche, but the theatre is an incredibly small world; and you may wind up auditioning for somebody who knew somebody whose show you *claim* you were in. If they start asking questions (usually out of genuine interest) like, "oh, I see you worked for so-and-so," and it comes out that you lied ... well, it looks bad. And it can cost you a job.

12. If you need some help preparing audition, ask a director.

If you feel you need another pair of experienced "eyes" to give you some feedback on your audition piece, don't hesitate to approach a director whom you know and trust. Ask if you can perform the piece for him/her and get some notes. This may help you give the piece the "polish" it needs to stand out from the rest of the pack.

13. Don't ever, *ever* apologize for your work.

Even if you think it was the worst audition you ever gave, don't make a face or roll your eyes, or in any other way indicate that you think your audition was awful to the auditors – all this kind of behavior does is show that you're insecure about yourself. Besides, for all you know, they might think yours was the best audition of the day! I know actors who got jobs after swearing it was the worst audition of their life, and others who felt it was their best – who never even got a callback.

14. Be ready.

Rehearse your piece (or pieces) so that you're ready to do it at the drop of a hat. You never know when an audition may come up, so you should always have a piece well-rehearsed and have it down cold so that there's no danger of forgetting your lines.

15. Just get up there and do it.

Don't stand up there for a long time taking deep breaths with your eyes closed, repeating some mantra, once you're in front of the auditors and you're getting all set to begin your piece. If you take forever to get ready, they're going to expect the brilliance of Brando by the time you finally begin to act, and no matter what you give them, they're liable to be disappointed after your dramatic build-up. Also, in most audition situations it's probably not a wise idea to bring tons of props with you. The auditors' time is usually limited, so don't devour too much of it by setting up tons and tons of props and describing the set. Remember, they want to see you *act*, not design a set.

16. Don't perform the piece directly *to* the auditors.

Unless they instruct you otherwise, I've found that most auditors prefer that you *not* direct your piece directly to them (i.e., as if they are the other character to whom you're doing the monologue). It tends to make them self-conscious and prevents them from being able to relax, sit back, and enjoy your work – because you're, in effect, turning the monologue into a scene and forcing them to be a part of it! Pick an imaginary spot of focus and direct the piece to that location (just make sure that spot is located so that the auditors can see your face clearly – don't put it upstage!).

17. Think about what message you are sending.

When you audition with a piece of your own choosing, you are telling the auditors something about yourself by what material you have selected. You are showing what your tastes are. Like it or not, it's true: women who get up there and do overtly sexual pieces are *sending a message*. Are you sure that's the message you want to be sending? If so, fine. So be it. But know this: how you present yourself will affect how you are cast, and how others look at you. Think carefully about the image you are presenting of yourself. Are you using the appropriate piece to send the image of yourself which you want to convey?

18. Have fun.

Why did we all get into the theatre to begin with? Because it's fun. Because we enjoy doing it. So, when you're the next one up to be called and you're nervous and your heart is pounding ... remember why you started acting in the first place. And when they say "Next!" – just go in there and try to have a good time.

Other Publications for Your Interest

PASTORAL
(COMEDY)
By PETER MALONEY

1 man, 1 woman—Exterior

Daniel Stern ("Blue Thunder", "Breaking Away") and Kristin Griffith ("The Europeans", "Interiors") starred originally at NYC's famed Ensemble Studio Theatre in the preceptive comedy about a city couple temporarily tending a farm. He hates the bucolic life and is terrified, for instance, by such horrors as a crowing rooster; whereas she is at one with the land *and* the rooster. "An endearing picture of young love at a comic crossroads."—N.Y. Times. "Sharp, satiric humor."—New Yorker. "An audience pleaser."—Village Voice. Published with *Last Chance Texaco*. (#17995)

LAST CHANCE TEXACO
(DRAMA)
By PETER MALONEY

3 women—Interior

Originally staged to great acclaim at NYC's famed Ensemble Studio Theatre, this is a haunting, lyrical play set in the American Garage, a Texaco station in a small Texas town run by a mother and her daughter. Late one night, while driving through, a city woman named Ruth has a flat tire, an occurrence which causes her own unusual life to intersect with Verna and Cissy, as they fix her tire in the American Garage. This play is an excellent source of monologue and scene material. It is also a gripping piece of theatre. Published with *Pastoral*. (#13887)

BUSINESSMAN'S LUNCH
(COMEDY)
By MICHAEL QUINN

4 men, 1 woman—Interior

Originally produced by the famed Actors Theatre of Louisville, this marked the debut of a wonderful new comic playwriting voice. We are in one of those quiche-and-salad restaurants, where three high-powered young executives of a nearby candy company are having lunch as they discuss company politics and various marketing and advertising strategies. They particularly enjoy making fun of one of their fellows who is not present, whom they consider a hopeless nerd—until, that is, they learn that he is engaged to marry the boss's daughter. "Cleverly skewers corporate stereotypes."—NY Times. (#4712)

Other Publications for Your Interest

SEASCAPE WITH SHARKS AND DANCER
(LITTLE THEATRE—DRAMA)

By DON NIGRO

1 man, 1 woman—Interior

This is a fine new play by an author of great talent and promise. We are very glad to be introducing Mr. Nigro's work to a wide audience with *Seascape With Sharks and Dancer*, which comes directly from a sold-out, critically acclaimed production at the world-famous Oregon Shakespeare Festival. The play is set in a beach bungalow. The young man who lives there has pulled a lost young woman from the ocean. Soon, she finds herself trapped in his life and torn between her need to come to rest somewhere and her certainty that all human relationships turn eventually into nightmares. The struggle between his tolerant and gently ironic approach to life and her strategy of suspicion and attack becomes a kind of war about love and creation which neither can afford to lose. In other words, this is quite an offbeat, wonderful love story. We would like to point out that the play also contains a wealth of excellent *monologue* and *scene material*.   (#21060)

GOD'S SPIES
(COMEDY)

By DON NIGRO

1 man, 2 women—Interior

This is a truly hilarious send-up of "Christian" television programming by a talented new playwright of wit and imagination. We are "on the air" with one of those talk shows where people are interviewed about their religious conversions, offering testimonials of their faith up to God and the Moral Majority. The first person interview by stalwart Dale Clabby is Calvin Stringer, who discourses on devil worship in popular music. Next comes young Wendy Trumpy, who claims to have talked to God in a belfry. Her testimonial, though, is hardly what Dale expected . . . Published with *Crossing the Bar*.   (#9643)

CROSSING THE BAR
(COMEDY)

By DON NIGRO

1 man, 2 women—Interior

Two women sit in a funeral parlor with the corpse of a recently-deceased loved one, saying things like "Doesn't he look like himself", when the corpse sits up, asking for someone named Betty. Who is this Betty, they wonder? God certainly works in mysterious ways . . . Published with *God's Spies*.   (#5935)

SPOON RIVER ANTHOLOGY

CHARLES AIDMAN

Conceived from EDGAR LEE MASTERS'
'Spoon River Anthology'

3 men, 2 women—A stage

Via musical interludes, we are introduced in a cemetery to the ghosts of those who were inhabitants of this town, and whose secrets have gone with them to the grave. There are 60-odd characterizations and vignettes in this constantly interesting entertainment, offering an amazingly varied array of roles and impersonations, from young lovers and preachers and teachers, to the funny chronicle of the poor mixed-up Jew who ends up in the wrong cemetery. Both the sordid and the humorous sides of life are portrayed, with fetching ballads, and the free verse form of Masters. "A dramatic presentation reduced to its simplest terms . . . moving and beautiful . . . an evening of astonishing stirring emotional satisfaction."—*N. Y. Post.* "A glowing theatre experience . . . a brooding and loving American folk poem brought to life on a stage."—*N. Y. Times.* "Vivid . . . quite an inspiration. . . . A decided novelty. . . . It has punch and humor and bitterness, and often it stabs the heart."—*N. Y. Daily News.* "Warm, radiant, poetic. . . . A compelling experience in the theatre."—*N. Y. Journal-American.* "A procession of unforgettable men and women, and a powerful evocation of life."—*N. Y. World-Telegram & Sun.*

DAVID and LISA

By JAMES REACH

Adapted from the book by THEODORE ISAAC RUBIN,
and the screenplay by ELEANOR PERRY

11 men, 11 women

The production is extremely simple; it is played against drapes and uses a minimum of props. The award-winning motion picture, *David and Lisa,* has now been adapted for the stage with the utmost fidelity to its illustrious prototype. It retells, by use of the most modern stage techniques, the strange, appealing and utterly fascinating story of the two mentally-disturbed adolescents: David, only son of wealthy parents, over-protected by a dominating mother, who is tortured by his mania against being touched; and Lisa, the waif who has never known parental love, who has developed a split personality and is in effect two different girls, one of whom will speak only in childish rhymes and insists upon being spoken to in the same manner. The play follows them during the course of one term at Berkley School, where they have come under the sympathetic and understanding guidance of psychiatrist Alan Swinford and his staff; follows them through exhilarating progress and depressing retrogression; follows them—and their fellow students: Carlos, the street urchin; the over-romantic Kate; stout Sandra, and others—with laughter and heartbreak and suspense.

Other Publications for Your Interest

TALKING WITH...
(LITTLE THEATRE)
By JANE MARTIN

11 women—Bare stage

Here, at last, is the collection of eleven extraordinary monologues for eleven actresses which had them on their feet cheering at the famed Actors Theatre of Louisville—audiences, critics and, yes, even jaded theatre professionals. The mysteriously pseudonymous Jane Martin is truly a "find"; a new writer with a wonderfully idiosyncratic style, whose characters alternately amuse, move and frighten us always, however, speaking to use from the depths of their souls. The characters include a baton twirler who has found God through twirling; a fundamentalist snake handler, an ex-rodeo rider crowded out of the life she has cherished by men in 3-piece suits who want her to dress up "like Minnie damn Mouse in a tutu"; an actress willing to go to any length to get a job; and an old woman who claims she once saw a man with "cerebral walrus" walk into a McDonald's and be healed by a Big Mac. "Eleven female monologues, of which half a dozen verge on brilliance."—London Guardian. "Whoever (Jane Martin) is, she's a writer with an original imagination."—Village Voice. "With Jane Martin, the monologue has taken on a new poetic form, intensive in its method and revelatory in its impact."—Philadelphia Inquirer. "A dramatist with an original voice . . . (these are) tales about enthusiasms that become obsessions, eccentric confessionals that levitate with religious symbolism and gladsome humor."—N.Y. Times. Talking With . . . is the 1982 winner of the American Theatre Critics Association Award for Best Regional Play.

(#22009)

If individual monologues are done separately: Royalty, $15-$10.)

HAROLD AND MAUDE
(ADVANCED GROUPS—COMEDY)
By COLIN HIGGINS

9 men, 8 women—Various settings

Yes: the Harold and Maude! This is a stage adaptation of the wonderful movie about the suicidal 19 year-old boy who finally learns how to truly live when he meets up with that delightfully whacky octogenarian, Maude. Harold is the proverbial Poor Little Rich Kid. His alienation has caused him to attempt suicide several times, though these attempts are more cries for attention than actual attempts. His peculiar attachment to Maude, whom he meets at a funeral (a mutual passion), is what saves him—and what captivates us. This new stage version, a hit in France directed by the internationally-renowned Jean-Louis Barrault, will certainly delight both afficionados of the film and new-comers to the story. "Offbeat upbeat comedy."—Christian Science Monitor.

(#10032)